The Western Frontier Library

[Complete list on page 165]

X. BEIDLER:

VIGILANTE

X. BEIDLER: VIGILANTE

Edited By
HELEN FITZGERALD SANDERS
in collaboration with
WILLIAM H. BERTSCHE, JR.
With a Foreword by
A. B. GUTHRIE, JR.

Norman
University of Oklahoma Press

978.6

B 39 X

35986

Feb. '58

Foreword

BY A. B. GUTHRIE, JR.

IN THE incredible story of banditry and Vigilante justice in the Montana of the 1860's few men are at once so well known and so little known as one X. Beidler. A Vigilante himself, he seems almost always to have been on hand when there were outlaws to catch or hang or both. References to him are frequent in the scant literature that has come down from those times, but they treat him usually as someone to be taken for granted. It is as if everyone, of course, knew X; nothing was needed other than the mention of his name.

Today's reader, unless in possession of rare and special information, is tantalized. What manner of man was he? How was it he was so often present when good men and true were wanted? Was his a dedication to the right or a disposition toward violence that just happened to find him on the side of right?

In 1880, not long after his biggest days, Beidler dictated parts of his experience to James Ponsford. From these words, here put in print, I can't say we get all the answers or any answer fully, but we do get ideas about the man. We get glimmerings and more than glimmerings. More, we get an eyewitness and participant's account of wild old times about which we've wanted to know more.

Beidler followed a variety of occupations—store clerk, prospector, pack train operator, freighter, deputy U. S. marshal, guard of gold shipments, collector of customs for Montana and Idaho. He first arrived at Alder Gulch in 1863.

X. Beidler: Vigilante

Wilbur Fisk Sanders, as courageous a prosecutor as ever faced a people's court, gives us a picture of him in a chronicle that is made a chapter of this book:

"One of the most noticeable, active and valuable men during its (the trial's) progress, was a diminutive, short, young man acting as guard, vigilant, supple, observant, now here and now there wherever anything was to be done to secure the orderly conduct of the affair. He carried as did a majority of the crowd, a shotgun, the muzzle of which stood up a few inches above his head."

Beidler himself leaves us largely to infer his character and disposition, for he was, or is in print, a matter-of-fact rather than a boastful or self-explaining man. But certain inferences seem safe from expressions like a few I will cite.

In Kansas, Beidler was with a party that ran a gang of border ruffians into a blacksmith shop. For want of lead the besiegers loaded a howitzer with printer's type and touched the fuse. Those not killed, he reports, "had to pick out the type from the persons of their comrades and that is the way they first learned to read."

Again, in speaking of a miners' court: "Those in favor of hanging were to go up hill and those in favor of no hanging were to go down hill and of course those in favor of no hanging were a lazy lot of loafers and naturally went down hill and beat us."

And still again: "The people around and in Virginia [City] were at this time in an excited state of mind, and I concluded to quit prospecting for gold and prospect for human fiends."

His language can be diverting, now marked by humor, now by figure of speech, now by that brevity with which old westerners even yet often spear a point.

"He took another smile out of the gin bottle. . . ."

Foreword

". . . when the hour given by the committee to Slade had expired Slade expired with it."

". . . my friend had fallen into the sleep of the innocents and snored like a band of Mormon wives."

Enough, except to add that, good as it is to have these recollections, we wish they could have been fuller.

Introduction

I BECAME INTERESTED in the Journal of John Xavier—better known as "X"—Beidler, when I was writing my *History of Montana*. I had done much research, with the co-operation of the Montana State Historical Society and other organizations, but I needed all the facts available and was convinced that the Beidler story might be a rich source of information.

"X" was a famous character in the Northwest, and my father-in-law, the late Colonel Wilbur F. Sanders, had told me of his daring exploits. They were two of the founders of the Vigilantes and worked together with their colleagues to crush Henry Plummer's notorious road gang and establish law and order in Montana territory. They were men of different types. Sanders was tall and lanky, Beidler short and stout. Sanders had a wife and child, Beidler was a lone wolf. Sanders had a brilliant mind and was a master of vitriolic oratory. Beidler, quick on the draw and rough, was essentially a man of action. However, he had a unique sense of humor, which, by a twist, could turn tragedy into comedy. He was merciless in the pursuit of criminals, but ready to risk his life to help those in need.

Sanders and Beidler first met at the trial of George Ives, a leader of the Plummer mob, for the brutal murder of Nicholas Tbolt, known as "the Dutchman." Ives had shot him in the back. Sanders, then a newcomer and young lawyer, had been appointed prosecuting attorney. He accepted the job realizing he might be a victim of the road agents. Ives was tried, found guilty, and sentenced to be hanged forthwith, by the miners' court. When the verdict was rendered, Ives made a touching appeal to Sanders, to urge the court to delay the execution until the following day, no doubt hoping that the Plummer gang would rescue him. The miners were emotional men, easily swayed by sentiment. After Ives spoke, there was a dramatic silence. Then from the roof of a log cabin, overlooking the scene, where "X" was perched, he shouted: "Ask him how long he gave the Dutchman!"

That settled the fate of George Ives.

Knowing these things, I felt certain that the "X." Beidler script would be helpful to me in writing my history, so I purchased it. I was not disappointed. "X" had dictated his story to James Ponsford in his later years and it was transcribed in longhand. The script was difficult to decipher and arrange in chronological order. As in the case of most such documents by uneducated men, the narrator and the copyist had little idea of sequence or continuity. It was a series of episodes which had to be put together like a jigsaw puzzle. I used some of this material in my *History of Montana*, but there was much I did not use and considered a valuable contribution to Americana. I edited the script carefully, deleting only a few passages which were irrelevant and vulgar. I made no attempt to tone down the vile language of the road agents, as some friendly critics advised me to do, because I felt it was the key to the character of evil men.

"X." Beidler died in Helena, Montana, in 1890, but his memory still lives. He has become almost a legendary figure in Northwestern history. He is buried in the blue shadow of the snowy Rocky Mountains and his grave is appropriately marked by a rough granite boulder, placed there by pioneers, whose watchword was: *"Men do your duty."*

HELEN FITZGERALD SANDERS

Publisher's Note

As MRS. SANDERS says in her introduction, arranging the original Beidler manuscripts for publication was something like piecing together the parts of a jigsaw puzzle. Included in the materials are Beidler's reminiscences as dictated in 1880 to James Ponsford, who transcribed them in longhand; newspaper clippings (often undated or unidentified as to source) and longhand copies of newspaper articles; accounts of certain incidents written by others, sometimes copied by Ponsford, sometimes in an unknown handwriting; and the story of George Ives, by Colonel Wilbur F. Sanders, who as a young attorney prosecuted Ives. Before publication, the materials were arranged chronologically (with the clippings and narratives by others filling the gaps in the Beidler account), broken into chapters, and repetitious or fragmentary portions deleted, although differences in reporting the same incident are noted. Appended to the book are miscellaneous comments and stories about Beidler, some anonymous, and an anonymous appreciation of Colonel Sanders. In the original longhand "journal," proper names sometimes are spelled in several different ways. These have been made consistent so far as possible and footnoted to indicate the variant spellings.

Contents

❖❖❖❖❖❖❖❖❖❖❖❖❖❖❖❖❖❖❖❖❖❖❖❖❖❖❖❖❖

Illustrations

X. BEIDLER:
VIGILANTE

[I]

Pennsylvania and Kansas

I WAS BORN in Mount Joy, Lancaster County, Pennsylvania, August 14th, 1831. Received a country school education. My mother was born in Germany and came to the U. S. when she was four years old, and my father was born in the U. S.

Moved to near Harrisburg upon a farm in 1838. The first pair of boots I got, I picked chestnuts and sold them for a "fippeny bit" a quart, and purchased the boots. I then picked hickory chips and sold them for $2.½ a load. Lived on the farm seven years and then wound up at Middletown, where my parents died and were buried.

On the morning of my father's death, I was coming up town to see the undertaker, and Simon Cameron asked me how father was. I told him he was dead and he told me I was shoved off the plank and would have to swim now—which I did not understand at the time.

About this time I was put to the shoemaking trade but I did not last at that business, and I got into the brick business in the summer, and broom making in the winter. I was making brick at Harrisburg and Middletown, then went to Chambersburg, Franklin County, into a hotel, as barkeeper and clerk. One summer I stayed near Gettysburg, at Caledonas Springs, then back to Chambersburg and made brick again the following summer.

My first and last Presidential election was at Harrisburg, in 1852, when I voted for General Scott for President. I then went to Atchison, Kansas, and made the first brick in that city.

3

X. Beidler: Vigilante

At that time the Kansas war was going on and I had to declare myself for free state or slavery, and I went for free state. On one occasion they sent me to Kickapoo to see about illegitimate voting and to see if I could stop it. The Kickapoo Rangers were running the polls. They voted me three or four times, then told me to pull out for Atchison, and gave me ten minutes to get. I got. Reported that I could do no good.

I did not make a success at brick making. My partners running off with the proceeds, left me broke. I wintered that year at Atchison and opened a place called "The People's Saloon," and ran that a while, and in '58 I started for Pike's Peak but did not get there and came back to Atchison.

While I was in Kansas, the border ruffians threw the printing press into the river at Lawrence, and left the type in the printing office, not knowing what type was for, or what use to make of it. We sacked up the type and took it with us. We pursued the ruffians to Hickory Point blacksmith shop and being short of shot but having plenty of powder, we utilized the type by loading our howitzer with it, putting it in oyster cans and ramming it home, and turned loose, pouring the type between the chinking of the first and second leg of the building. A great quantity struck the ruffians immediately below the spinal column. Those that were not wounded in this manner, had to pick out the type from the persons of their comrades and that is the way they first learned to read. We finally dislodged them by getting a load of hay and smoking them out.

In the winter of '58 I was in Atchison, Kansas, and the U. S. Marshal from Lawrence was after John Brown. On a Sunday he sent in to Atchison for a posse to help arrest John Brown, who was running nigger slaves through from Missouri to Nebraska. Doc Hereford, William Green, a Mr. Budd and

4

a Dutchman, were about all that could be got to help arrest John Brown. I had a very kind invitation to go along but I didn't have time. They went out and found Brown camped on a slough, and he, with his niggers, held up the Marshal and his whole posse, capturing four or five of them, and held them for trial and put a nigger guard over them, while they deliberated whether to hang, shoot, or drown them. It was left to a vote and it came to a tie and Brown had the deciding vote. He voted to let them go, then when the prisoners had been liberated, Doc Hereford got up to thank Capt. John Brown for the mercy he had extended in saving their lives.

Capt. Brown said: "Now go home boys—go to Atchison and don't hunt any more for John Brown. He is not lost."

Then Hereford and the party wanted their horses, arms, etc., when Capt. Brown says: "Why, boys, I always thought such things were spoils of war. You declared war on me and I captured you and your horses. I need horses. I will send you home on the cactus [prickly pear] line."

Doc Hereford said: "Well, Capt. Brown, let us have our weapons, then."

"You have no weapons here," answered Brown.

"Why," said Hereford, "we had our guns and pistols and you captured them and have them now."

"O!" said Brown, "when I took them they were mine and the boys'. I will not give them to you, as you will not need them on your way home. You will not meet John Brown and if you did, you would not fight him."

They came home to Atchison, glad to get back and declared they wanted no more John Brown in theirs. They looked rough but every one of them had a good word for old Capt. John Brown.

On the 1st day of November, Capt. John Brown was brought

5

into court to receive the sentence of death. Here is his last speech:

"I have, may it please the Court, a few words to say. In the first place, I deny everything but what I have all along admitted—the design on my part to free the slaves.

"I intended certainly, to have made a clear thing of that matter, as I did last winter, when I went to Missouri and there took slaves without the snapping of a gun on either side, moved them through the country and finally left them in Canada.

"I designed to have done the same thing again, on a larger scale. That was all I intended. I never did intend murder, or treason, or the destruction of property, or to excite or to incite slaves to rebellion, or to make insurrection.

"I have another objection; and that is it is unjust that I should suffer such a penalty. Had I interfered in the manner in which I admit, and which I admit has been fairly proved— for I admire the truthfulness and candor of the greater portion of the witnesses who have testified in this case—had I so interfered in behalf of the rich, the powerful, the intelligent, the so-called great, or in behalf of any of their friends, either father, mother, brother, sister, wife or children—or any of that class and suffered and sacrificed what I have in this interference, it would have been all right, and every man in this Court would have deemed it an act worthy of reward rather than punishment.

"This Court acknowledges, as I suppose, the validity of the Law of God, I see a book kissed here, which I suppose to be the Bible, or at least the New Testament, and teaches me that all things 'whatsoever I would that men should do unto me, I should do even so to them.'

"I endeavored to act up to that instruction. I say that I am too young yet to understand that God is any respector of

6

persons. I believe that to have interfered as I have done, as I always freely admitted I have done, in behalf of His despised poor was not wrong, but right. Now if it is deemed necessary that I should forfeit my life for the furtherance of the ends of justice, and mingle my blood further with the blood of my children and with the blood of millions in this slave country, whose rights are disregarded by wicked, cruel, and unjust enactments—I submit: so let it be done.

"Let me say one word further: I feel entirely satisfied with the treatment I have received at my trial. Considering all the circumstances, it has been more generous than I expected, but I feel no consciousness of guilt. I have stated from the first what was my intention and what was not, I never had any design against the life of any person nor any disposition to commit treason, or excite slaves to rebel, or make any general insurrection. I never encouraged any man to do so, but always discouraged any idea of that kind.

"Let me say also, a word in regard to the statements made by some of those connected with me. I hear it has been said by some of them that I have induced them to join me. But the contrary is true. I do not say this to injure them, but as regretting their weakness. There is not one of them but joined me of his own accord and the greater part, at their own expense. A number of them I never saw and never had a word of conversation with until the day they came to me, and that was for the purpose I have stated.

"Now I have done."

[II]

Colorado Rescue

IN AN OVERLAND LETTER, written on the Plains in May, 1859, Mr. Horace Greely said: "I believe I have now descended the ladder of artificial life nearly to its lowest round. If the Cheyennes—thirty of whom stopped the last Express down on the route we must traverse, and tried to beg or steal from it—should see fit to capture and strip us, we should of course, have further experience in the same line, but for the present the progress I have made during the last fortnight towards the primitive simplicity of human existence may be roughly noted thus:

"May 12th—Chicago—Chocolate and morning newspapers last seen on the breakfast table.

"May 23rd—Leavenworth—Room bells and baths make their last appearance.

"May 24th—Topeka—Beefsteak and wash bowls (other than tin) last visible. Barber ditto.

"May 26th—Manhattan—Potatoes and eggs last recognized among the blessings that brighten as they take their flight.

"May 27th—Junction City—Last visitation of a boot-black, with dissolving views of a broad bedroom. Chairs bid us goodbye.

"May 28th—Pipe Creek—Benches for seats at meals have disappeared, giving place to bags and boxes. We (two passengers of a scribbling turn) write our letters in the Xpress wagon that has borne us by day and must supply us lodgings for the night."

Colorado Rescue

Early in the spring of 1859 I started for where Denver is now. Crossing Blue River, Frank Marshall, brother-in-law, killed two men who had refused to pay their toll, which caused quite an excitement. We proceeded on with our train and arrived at Denver in May. That summer I worked for Fenton and Hall in their store. That was the summer Greely came out and gave us a talk. I carried his report down the Platte River to the California crossing, near where Julesburg is now. That report was the cause of a great many emigrants coming West.

While I was in Denver in '59 and '60, I saw the duel between Dick Whitsit and Park McClure. Also the duel between Lew Bliss and Doc Stone. This fight was for blood all the way through, the contestants using double barreled shotguns and ounce balls. Bliss killed his man.

When Mose Young killed old man West at Denver, Sam How and myself arrested Mose Young upstairs over Richard's store. He was hid under a pile of old mule harness. He was tried and hung on the bank of Cherry Creek. Young and West both came from Leavenworth together, and Young's trial by the people only lasted a couple of hours.

Between Washington and California Gulch in '60, a lot of miners went prospecting and when about 50 miles west of California Gulch, we ran into a band of Apaches. Eight white men were killed, the white men having killed their own horses to use for barricades. Sometime after this fight, we came along and found the dead men decomposed and full of arrows. We buried them in as decent shape as possible. This was on Eagle Creek, between Washington and California Gulches, where Leadville is now. In traveling the gulch afterwards, we found that the wolves had dug up the bodies, and the skulls and bones were scattered around. We re-buried them. We

9

picked up what relics we could and put the bones all in one mound and I hear it is there at this day. This place we called the Dead Man's Gulch and it is known by that title to this day.

I was running a pack train at this time, with a couple of hired men and this little incident made us keep our eyes open and look out for Indians.

At Taylor River an Indian came to my camp one evening looking pretty hard up,—looked as if he had nothing to eat for some time, and bow and arrows. I fed him, took care of him and gave him his breakfast. In the morning after breakfast, he lit out. I think he was an Apache, Comanche, or Navajo. He left camp and I was making about 15 miles a day. I went into camp that evening and he came into my camp again. I fed him supper again and took care of him in the morning. He got up and after breakfast I gave him a big lunch to carry him a long way off. That day I made another 15 or 20 mile drive. That Indian came back to my camp again—third time—then I got tired. We had some picks and shovels along and we dug a hole and placed him and his horse into it after killing them. We had to bury everything belonging to this Indian, as he was packing information to the Indians as to our whereabouts and they were going to get even. We then dug another hole, six feet from this grave,—throwing all the dirt on the top of the place where this Indian and his horse and traps were buried, thus obliterating all traces of the death and burial of the Indian. The Indians afterwards hunted for their man but never found him. The prospect hole we dug alongside of the grave fooled them.

In 1861, in the Fall, at Denver, Jim Gordon killed a German through a little difficulty about a cow. The parties in the Saloon had been gambling and Gordon called his friends up to drink, while they were drinking the little German stepped up and said: "Mr. Gordon, I will take a drink with you."

"No," Gordon said, "you stole a cow out of my corral and you stand back there. These are gentlemen drinking. Now wait."

Gordon pushed the German away and he came back again, when Gordon grabbed the German by the top of his head, pulled his pistol and shot him through the crown of his head. The German died instantly. Gordon started for home and stopped in a lumber yard. No one could go near him but Jim Latta, whose gun he had killed the German with. They went to a big, lone tree and Latta got a horse for Gordon to escape with, leading the horse through town covered with a blanket letting on the horse was sick. He gave Gordon $25 and turned him loose. Gordon went to Boulder City and back to Denver to his own ranche. Took a mare belonging to Latta. Gordon did not seem to comprehend that he had killed anyone and sent Bill Clark up to Denver to see how the land lay. Bill found that Gordon had killed the man, returned and started Gordon off for safety, and stated that the citizens of Denver were in arms against him. Gordon went to A. J. Williams, Ft. Lampton, 25 miles below Denver, where he was corralled but escaped in a running fight under a heavy fire, but escaped again. He then went for Latta's camp on Cherry Creek, barefooted. There he got a mule and a pair of boots and rode 80 miles away to Fort Smith on the Arkansas River. Got some new clothes which Jim Latta paid for to a stranger. This stranger went to the Deputy Marshal Meadows[1] and reported where Gordon was. They started after him and he was captured in Coffee County, Kansas. They took him to Leavenworth where the Germans were incensed against him but he

[1] Beidler sometimes calls him "Deputy Marshall Meadow."

was tried and discharged. They dragged him from the jail to the Planter's Hotel but were not admitted. Then the Sheriff cleared the road and took the prisoner back to the gaol for safety. He then surrendered himself to Meadows for trial at Denver, where he was tried and convicted and hung in the daytime by the people. This Deputy Marshal Meadows was afterwards killed,—being caught monkeying with another man's wife,—being killed by her husband. It was reported that Jim Gordon's friends killed Meadows, but there is nothing in it and it is not true.

Jim Latta was arrested as an accomplice in the Gordon tragedy but was discharged, as there was no evidence against him and he was innocent and Jim thinks it was a close call. Jim says he was as innocent as a lamb. Plenty of people who did not know the facts, blamed J. Latta as being an accomplice and do to this day, but I know he is innocent.

In August '61 in Colorado at California Gulch in company with Al Nichols, we started out and made a night camp at Twin Lakes, the prettiest place on earth at that time. In the morning we pulled out and saw a mountain sheep away up on the mountain which Al Nichols shot with his rifle and just as Al killed the sheep another man, not with us, shot and the two rifles went off together. We started up after our sheep and the other party started too, thinking he had killed the sheep. We agreed that when we got the sheep we could decide who had killed it as the other man's gun took an ounce ball and Al's one half the size. We climbed up the mountain and found that the ounce ball didn't get there, and we also found the mountain sheep frozen almost solid. Upon measuring the distance back, we found it to be away over half a mile and almost straight up which accounted for the sheep freezing.

I told Al he must have strained his gun and wouldn't give him a cent for it after that shot.

We crossed the Lake Range after that and also crossed Taylor River. Al had an old brindle cow along which followed us around like a dog and at every creek or river Al used to ride the cow across and she came in very handy at night—giving a large amount of milk.

We camped at Rock creek and here was a party of three brothers named Hezekia, Obadia, and Jacobia Dopp,—three of the meanest rats I ever met. We asked them to help pack our meat, thinking they would do so as they had empty saddles but they firmly refused. My poor Jacks had at least 250 lbs. on each, but when we got to camp these Dopps were the first to come and get a choice cut off our sheep and some milk from the old brindle cow, which we gave them.

Among our outfit we had a couple of gallons of the best whisky we could find in the Gulch, and as is usual with packers, as soon as the animals were turned loose and saddles and blankets fixed, all hands took a drink.

We unpacked and were going to irrigate, when up comes one of the Dopp boys (Hezekia) with a tin cup in his hand and he would like some of that. I filled his cup to take to his camp. When he got the cup full he said: "If we only had a cup full for morning!"

This made me hot. He had refused the only favor we asked him, and then wanted pretty near our whole outfit.

Two days after, while going down the mountain, one of our Jack-packs missed his footing and rolled down the side of the mountain and we certainly thought he would not have a whole bone in his body, but when Al and I got to where the animal was, we found it lying on its side, eating some of the luxuriant grass and acting as if nothing had happened.

13

X. Beidler: Vigilante

We got to our journey's end, Washington Gulch, and found a prosperous mining camp.

I returned to California Gulch and Al stayed at Washington Gulch.

Al's pack animal on this trip was his old brindle cow, and it used to take him all this time watching her, as the boys all carried tin cups, and if Al was caught away, Old Brin, as we used to call her, had to give up. Milk was a luxury at that time, especially to packers, and Al had to give us our rations morning and night.

On my way back to Denver with the train, I met an old Irish gentleman, with his son about 20 years old. The old man was afoot and broke and hungry, so was his son,—the old man $\frac{1}{4}$ mile ahead of the boy. He wanted something to eat. I provided him with bacon and flour. I asked him the cause of his distress. He said he had been up to Cherry Creek Gold Mines and had found no gold and with what little means he had left he built a skiff and loaded it with grub enough to go home on, and they run onto a little Beaver dam and the dam' Beaver took them in on their way down. They waded ashore and started afoot home. I asked him why an old gentleman his age should start out gold mining. He said his lad wanted to go and his wife would not let him unless he went along to take care of him. It learned the lad never to go gold-seeking again.

I was then put in charge of the bull train, Mr. Fenton being alkalied. I went to the South Park diggings the following spring, on my own hook. Louis Dubois and Mark Taylor, Dick Dunn and an old German, Jake Readin, who is in Cooke City now, and very rich, was also along. He had an old mule and cart along. The mule would run down every hill but we had to pull him and his load up every hill. We left Tarryall diggins and went across the range to Blue River country dig-

14

Montana State Historical Society

Early photograph of John X. Beidler

gins we found, and here we had to make snowshoes. We took up placer claims and went to digging. I sunk $500 and never got a color, or lowered the river an inch.

Came back to Denver and got a pair of mules and wagon and loaded up with boots for California Gulch and sold them at my own price, everybody making money. I then purchased pack animals and started a pack train. Furnished Humbug and Georgia Gulches and Swan River and Delaware Flats with things most needed. I ran the first pack train into Washington Gulch, near where Gunnison is now and in the winter there was not enough grub to keep all hands.

There was a family by the name of Jones,—his wife and two children. The snow was 3 to 5 feet deep. I was ten days coming 100 miles with this family. I lost several animals on the trip. Several old Montanians were with me in that trip, including George Krattcer, Bob Coburn, and George Cleveland. Every evening we had to shovel snow down to the grass to get the animals something to eat. We camped on the snow, cutting limbs from the trees and laying them down on the snow to hold us up, and the fire was 'way below us towards morning. In the spring, when we went back, we found the places where we had cut the limbs off the trees 20 to 30 feet from the ground, which seems pretty loud, but it is the truth all the same, and Marshal who was along, wanted to know how it occurred. The only misfortune we had in rescuing this family was the little girl got one foot frozen. When we got to the top of the range and within 1½ miles of our camp, the snow got too soft for the animals to travel. I took all the pack saddles, blankets etc., and made them into a bundle and slid them down to the foot of the range, out of the deep snow. I then started the mules down and they slid down safely and in great shape until they got to good footing. The

boys went ahead and rustled grub from California Gulch,—
we being out,—and came back and met us at the foot of the
mountain.

[*Krattcer's account of the trip:*]

In the latter part of November 1861 myself and others, J. X.
Beidler being one of the party, camped in Washington Gulch,
Colorado. I had been there during the summer, and at this
time X made a proposition to take a bear hunt. Our party
started out on the proposed hunt and were out five days, it
finally proving to be a *bare* hunt. It was bad and stormy; the
storm lasting so long that we pulled out for camp. And after
we arrived in camp X came to me and says: "Uncle George,
there is a family here, known as the Jones family, that will
have to go out of this place."

The family consisted of man and wife and one grown son
by his former wife, and one son and one daughter by his
present wife. And X says (who was more ready to help others
than to help himself): "Uncle George, I want you to go with
me and help get them over the range to California Gulch."

So we formed a party of eight men to assist the family over
the range, a distance of eighty miles. It had been snowing
five days and was still snowing, this being the 3rd of December. The snow at that time was three feet on the level.
On this day, the third, we traveled three miles, this being
the start of our journey. On the 4th we traveled to the mouth
of the canyon known as the California Canyon, making our
day's travel the distance of nine miles. Camped there and on
the morning of the 5th X came to me again and made the
remark that we were getting along too slowly as it was still
snowing. He proposed that I should take a number of the best
animals, the woman and her children and go ahead. He would
bring up the rear with the poorest animals. So I selected

X. Beidler: Vigilante

Henry Kern's mule for the woman and little girl to ride, and the noted mule, Black Bess, to carry the woman's feather bed and bedding and Robert Coburn's sorrel horse and my bay mare for myself and Lee Halley. Joe had one cow in the outfit and we packed a part of the house plunder on her, and she proved to be an unworthy animal and stampeded, scattering her burden in the snow. We got saddled up and I moved out leaving X and party behind, and also Jones to manage the cow.

We traveled that day until about three o'clock and we struck Dead Man's Gulch (which derived its name from a party of men having been murdered there by the Indians). Our camp was about seventy-five yards from the place where X had found those murdered men. There we encountered a Northwester and had to camp. We ran some canvas around some trees (as we had noticed) to make a place to keep the woman and children from freezing to death. The men put in their time building fires, and between fires, shoveled snow to get grass for the animals. X and party camped about four miles behind us.

On the morning of the 6th it was too cold for the woman and children to travel. X passed us and traveled on, but our animals being so much stronger and more able, we overtook them in the evening and we all camped together that night on Rock Creek.

We also put in our time that night shoveling snow, and building fires. Caught a nap whenever we could, leaning up against a tree.

On the morning of the 7th I took the lead again, but we traveled together for a short distance when X sent a man on in advance to tell me to go ahead; not to wait on him as some of his animals were about to give out and he would have to camp, or go slower. So I moved on about a mile, when Jones led the mule his wife was riding across a stream. Giving the mule a jerk, it threw the woman off in the water, she getting as wet as water could make her. She had to travel the rest of that day with her wet clothes. We camped that night in a little park, after traveling through a long strip of timber, taking the most of the day to get through it.

On the morning of the 8th day the sun rose clear and we packed our animals and started. Our camp was about six miles from the foot of the range which we arrived at about one o'clock. We concluded then to try to cross the range that evening. We proceeded on our way about three miles and Black Bess gave out with her burden, and also the cow got wearied out and refused to go any farther. We left the cow and Bess at that point in charge of Jones. And as the woman's saddle mule gave out with carrying her double burden (the woman and little girl) we relieved the mule by Harrison Jones (the young man) carrying the little girl; the little boy carried Lee Halley's gun and Halley carried the woman's feather bed. We had to pick our trail around on the crags to keep out of the deepest snow and finally reached the summit at five o'clock in the evening.

On going down the side of the range we had some trouble with the animals. The mule that the woman was riding was tired out so it could not carry her any farther. Harrison, his little brother, a man we called Frenchy, and the little girl had gone on ahead to the nearest point of timber three miles away, and to have a fire when we got there, if we could get there at all.

I left Halley, Coburn and Kern with the animals, and went on with the woman to try to make camp. We had no other conveyance but had to walk (as our animals had all given out). The woman got wearied out and sat down and begged me to go on and leave her, as she said she could never get to camp, but I encouraged her and after her giving out and sitting down three times and begging me to go on and leave her, I aided her all I could and we finally reached camp between eight and nine o'clock. Kern, Halley and Coburn reached camp shortly afterwards and Jones about an hour afterward, but he left the cow and mule on the range.

On the evening of the 9th when we broke camp, Jones went after the cow which I knew would go back to the last camping place to get water. After we were through, realizing the danger of being caught on the range in the night in a storm, I sent a note back to X, or for Jones to post up on the trail, so X would see it, for him not to try to cross the range unless he had all day to do it in. As good luck would have it X got the note. Jones got his cow and Black Bess over the range, but had to leave Bess at the foot of the range, where X found her the day following. Jones trudged on with the cow to overtake us. That morning my party and I started, traveled on that day and reached the place called the Twin Lake House that evening, a distance of twenty miles, without any mishap. We were all thankful that our lives had been spared to see a house once more.

On the morning of the 10th myself and Coburn gathered up some fresh animals that X had at this Twin Lake House, and as we knew X and party were short of provisions, we procured some of the animals and provisions for him and his party. Then we started back to meet them, which we succeeded in doing near the foot of the range, both parties striking camp nearly the same time that day. We found X and party in great need of our supplies.

On the 11th we all made it safely back to the Twin Lake House, and after staying there a day or two, we all scattered, every one taking his own course.

This was as bold and good hearted a lot of men as was ever

my lot to be cast among. And if this should meet with the eyes of any of that party please address me at Bozeman, Montana.

G. W. Krattcer.

That winter I [Beidler] went to Canon City and stayed there until spring, and returned to California Gulch and Denver where I outfitted to start for Montana Territory in company with John Grannis and George Berhingen, both of Gallatin City.

[III]

The Murders of Dillingham and Tbolt

In 1863 when Alder Gulch was first discovered, I, in company with John Grannis and J. Berhinger, took up three claims in Highland District. There was a big stampede at the time from all parts of the world. We had started in to clear our ground of brush, when a big Irishman jumped Grannis's claim. Berhinger hollered to me from his claim that Grannis's was jumped. I told him to hold on to his. A fellow came to me and ordered me off, but I stood him off and told him I was chief and would camp there. He left me. We divided with Grannis afterwards.

We started a drain ditch and there was lots of work of the kind I did not like. I stood it about 10 days in the water and then I looked after the horses—got supplies, etc., for camp and done chores.

During the time this [Montana] Territory was without law, the miners of Bannack had a miners' court, over which Judge Burchett presided. Henry Plummer, notorious as a road agent, was at that time Sheriff of Beaverhead, the only organized county in the Territory. The robber gang was thoroughly organized while the miners were not. Plummer had appointed members of his band as deputies for all the country now known as Montana. They did pretty much as they pleased, murdering and robbing promiscuously throughout the territory. Plummer even aspired to be Marshal of the Territory, and forwarded his application to Washington. His commission came on after he had been hung.

The Murders of Dillingham and Tbolt

One of the first murders in the territory was committed by Pete Horan, who killed an old man named Keeler. Plummer arrested Horan, an accomplice of his, who, after trial, was sentenced to be hanged. Horan managed to escape from his guards and ran to a creek, but was shortly afterwards recaptured and again taken into court. Judge Burchett was notified. He appeared, with the Court docket under his arm, took a seat in the room, threw one leg leisurely over a table, took a chew of tobacco and then said: "Well, Pete, you tried to get away, I hear."

Pete admitted that he had.

"Well," said the Judge, "it seems to me you should have known better than that. We won't let you go but will hang you damned quick. In just three hours you may make up your mind to be hung."

Pete pleaded in vain for an extension of sentence, but the Judge was inexorable.

The prisoner then sent for Jerry Sullivan, whom he knew to be a Catholic, stated he was also a Catholic and that he would like to see a Priest before he died.

There was no Priest nearer than the Bitter Root Valley, but Mr. Sullivan went to Judge Burchett, and endeavored to have the execution postponed three days, saying by that time he would have a priest here.

Judge Burchett would not consent to a postponement, and so Mr. Sullivan returned to Pete and told him he must prepare to meet his fate, that a Priest could not be had.

"But I'll tell you what it is Pete," said he, "you just get down on your knees, sir, and pray for forgiveness, sir, and I'll be damned if I don't think your sins will be forgiven, sir."

Pete was hanged promptly at the time stated.

Plummer built the gallows for Horan's execution and was himself hanged thereon.

X. Beidler: Vigilante

One day when I was down in Virginia City after meat for supper, Jack Gallagher came to me to borrow my mare to go down the Gulch. I refused. He wanted to know what was the matter with me. I told him I had to get back to camp with meat for supper for the boys. He insisted on me letting him take the animal for a short time, to which I finally consented. He promised to be back in 30 minutes but was gone 2 hours and a half. When he came back I was boiling, you bet, and indignant into the bargain and I called him some pretty hard names. He told me to go slow but I told him I hadn't time and that the next time he wanted a horse from me he wouldn't get it. He said: "Why, I will set you afoot."

I told him there was no one holding him.

A few days previous to this George Ives took a mule of mine, Black Bess, up to the Firehole country but said nothing to me about it. I found the mule all sweated and raised a fuss about it and Ives said it was the best mule in Montana and he knew because he had rode it 75 miles a day for several days. I told him if ever I caught him on an animal of mine I would kill him. He told me to put my animals on a ranche or take them away from there.

Ives and Tex Crowell came to this place 10 days after I had camped there, and ordered me to take my animals away, or he would for me.

I told him I could go to the Gulch and get a lot of miners and clean them out. He got very angry and he instructed his herder to take the lariats off my saddle animal.

I went to his lodge and found my lariat among his own and took it home with me.

Met Ives and Tex Crowell and a lot of the gang with Gallagher in the pot.

George Ives came to me and said: "Do you know who I am?"

The Murders of Dillingham and Tbolt

I said: "Yes, I think you are a horse thief from the way you have acted."

We went into a place and took a drink—I paid for it—at the same time telling them I did not care who they were. I was still hot at Gallagher and he at me, about him riding my mare. I then found out that the object of Gallagher's getting my mare was to make arrangements to murder J. W. Dillingham, who was Deputy Sheriff under Plummer, which they (Charley Forbes, Buck Stinson and Haze Lyons) successfully accomplished at the foot of Main Street, Virginia City, while Dr. Steele[1] was holding a miners' court.

Dillingham was a Philadelphian, a fine looking young fellow, about 26 years old and finely educated. He was one of Plummer's Deputies, but he had no sympathy with the gang.[2]

One evening in June at Bannack, in 1863, he accidentally overheard Buck Stinson, Haze Lyons and Charley Forbes,[3] three other deputies of Plummer, plotting to murder a man named Dodge, who intended to leave Bannack the next day with some $2,000 in gold dust for Virginia City, then a new camp, with a view of buying a claim. Their plan was to meet Dodge at Rattlesnake Creek, fifteen miles from Bannack, and there murder and rob him.

Dillingham hastily sought out Dodge, with whom he was acquainted, and notified him of his danger. Dodge was an honest, unsuspecting fellow and paid little attention to the warning. The next day he started for Virginia with his money, but when he reached Rattlesnake Creek, sure enough there were Buck Stinson, Haze Lyons and Charley Forbes. Dodge was well acquainted with the trio and gave them a cordial

[1] Beidler sometimes spells this name "Steel."

[2] The following account of the murder of Dillingham and the trial of his murderers is taken in part from the Beidler journals, in part from quotations from Beidler in the *Helena Independent* (1882).

[3] Beidler sometimes refers to him as "Ford."

25

greeting. Still unsuspecting his peril, he jocularly remarked that Dillingham had told him the night before that they intended to meet him at Rattlesnake and murder him for his money. The robbers exchanged rapid glances. It was evident that Dillingham had "blowed" up on them and if they dared to carry out their design they would be known as the murderers of Dodge.

Dodge's thoughtless remark saved his life, but sealed the fate of poor Dillingham.

They proceeded to Virginia City and a few days afterwards Dillingham also arrived there. No sooner had he reached there than the robber gang was notified.

Dr. W. L. Steele, now one of Helena's most popular physicians, was presiding over a miners' court in Virginia City, the temple of justice being a small willow wickiup, temporarily erected for the occasion. Here Buck Stinson, Haze Lyons, and Charley Forbes assembled the morning after Dillingham arrived and waited for his appearance upon the street. Soon Dillingham was seen to approach. The desperadoes slipped to the door and shot him down. This occurred about the 20th of June, 1863.

Dillingham was dead, lying in a brush wickiup on a gambling table. We arrested his murderers. They were tried. Doc Steele was President of the meeting. That night we held them prisoners in a log cabin near Dorris' store—we had to take chains and padlocks to secure them—having no handcuffs.

We ironed one when the balance bucked and said they would die before we should put chains on them. I told them it was good to die.

The captain of the guard said: "Pull down on them boys!" when they thought they had better take their medicine and take chains instead of lead, which chains we put on with pleasure and they made us feel more secure.

The Murders of Dillingham and Tbolt

There was a bad crowd hovering around, and no one could tell when a rumpus would commence. Buck Stinson, one of the prisoners, was a deputy sheriff under Plummer—so was Jack Gallagher and Dick Todd, and we had to stand stiff-legged against such a gang.

In the morning we went to trial with the prisoners, before the miners in the open air. Judge H. P. A. Smith and Jim Thurmond were attorneys for the prisoners. Testimony was taken in reference to the murder, and Charley Forbes, whose true name was Richardson, got up to make his own plea before the court and people. He was a bright, handsome young fellow and a capital talker. He claimed that his pistol did not go off and worked upon the sympathies of the jury by his pathetic references to his mother and other members of his family, that he was acquitted, while Haze Lyons and Buck Stinson were convicted.

Buck Stinson and Haze Lyons were sentenced to death by vote of the people, who had listened attentively to all testimony for and against.

Dick Sapp and myself were ordered to build a scaffold and see that the graves were dug. We worked like Beavers to get some forked trees from the Cottonwoods; built the scaffolds and started in to build the graves. When finished, we came down after the prisoners to hang them and found a big crowd of excited people—about two thousand miners. We put the two condemned men into a wagon to haul them to the place of execution.

The hour of execution arrived—a bright summer evening —and the miners gathered at the place on a sloping hillside, to witness the first hanging in Montana.

We had built the scaffold and dug the graves. The condemned men were seated in a wagon and surrounded by a guard.

27

X. Beidler: Vigilante

But the confederates of the doomed men had not been idle. Jack Gallagher and George Ives bustled through the crowd. At the final moment Gallagher announced that he held in his hand a farewell letter which young Haze Lyons had written that day to his mother. He then proceeded to read it in a deep, sonorous voice. The letter was beautifully written and evidently prepared by Lyons, allowing for effect. It contained tender reminiscences of his boyhood, loving messages to his mother, and a most touching farewell.

There were three ladies in attendance, the only women in Virginia, and they shed tears copiously as the letter was read. They begged for mercy for the doomed prisoners. The rough men of the wilderness, unused to the sight of feminine sorrow, were visibly affected.

C. Forbes, who was acquitted, lit out and didn't want to take any chances.

As we were about to start, Jack Gallagher got up and called for a new vote on the hanging and all in favor of letting the prisoners go in the crowd of two thousand miners were to hold up their right hands. It was impossible to decide which side had it. I then called for a new vote. It was agreed upon to have two men—one to take the hang men and one to take the no hang men, and see who had the best of it. The men who voted had to pass between these two men and declare themselves hang, or no hang, and the vote counted after all had passed through—stood no hang.

We kicked because the desperadoes turned loose and done as fine a piece of electioneering as was ever done in the world, voting as often as they could pass through.

Then another proposition was made by the toughs. Those in favor of hanging were to go up hill and those in favor of no hanging were to go down hill and of course those in favor of no hanging were a lazy lot of loafers and naturally went down hill and beat us.

A few of us said that the prisoners had been tried and convicted and must be hung. Our voices were drowned in the tumult and clamor and the immense multitude, almost unanimously, moved down hill, leaving some two hundred of us on the upper side of the slope.

George Ives took advantage of this and moved to set aside the verdict of the miners' jury and to discharge the prisoners. Jack Gallagher got up and declared (with six-shooters in his hands) the prisoners acquitted. He was a deputy sheriff and it had its effect on the crowd. A great many of the miners got disgusted and left for their claims. A wild yell that shook the side of the mountain, broke from all the crowd as the prisoners were released. The murderers were acquitted and poor Dillingham lay dead, murdered in cold blood, laying on a gambling table in a willow wickiup. The roughs had carried the day.

Virginia City seemed to be turned into a perfect Pandemonium, filled with the wild revelry of the robber band and their friends. Placards were stuck upon the streets bearing these words: "GRAVES TO LET," referring to the two empty graves which I had dug for the prisoners that day.

Judge Smith came to me and asked me why Dillingham was not buried. I told him I had been pretty busy digging graves and putting up scaffolds but that I had time now.

I got a few friends together and proposed that we at least give poor Dillingham decent burial. I made a coffin and dug a grave and just at twilight, a sad and silent, but meager procession formed line and followed the corpse through the boisterous streets. It was a dramatic scene—the sorrowing few—moving to the grave surrounded by general revelry—the dying twilight lingering upon the peaks around Virginia

City, while the deepening gloom slowly enveloped the valleys and crept up the mountain side, as if driving before it the fading glories of the day. The sun was hiding its head as if in shame. Night and lawlessness were triumphant.

When Buck Stinson and Haze Lyons were sentenced to be hung, Barton's wife and daughter and two other ladies created considerable sympathy for the prisoners by their tears and this was one of the reasons for their acquittal. When on our way to the grave of Dillingham we passed by Barton's cabin. He said to me: "The tears of my wife and daughter saved the lives of those poor boys from being hung."

I said: "I notice that they have no tears of sympathy for this dead man, who was murdered by those dear boys in cold blood."

At the grave there was no one to offer up a prayer. Just as we lowered the body, Judge H. P. A. Smith approached the grave.

"Judge Smith," I said bitterly, "you have had your triumph today. You have saved your clients, the murderers. Leave us to bury their victim."

Smith seemed touched with sorrow. Tears—probably whiskey tears—came to his eyes and dropping on his knees by the open grave, he exclaimed: "Let us pray."

We bowed our heads while he poured out a prayer for the dead man and his beloved ones, that for fervency and pathos has never been equalled in Montana.

This was the last triumph of the road agents.

At this time Bivin's Gulch was discovered about 15 miles north of Virginia City and a stampede there took place, and in company with Dr. Steele and other miners we started to follow the discoverers of the new gulch. Had to strike matches to keep on the trail, not knowing the country as well as they did.

Montana State Historical Society

Virginia City, Montana Territory, photographed probably in 1866

X. Beidler: Vigilante

Got into the Gulch about daylight in the morning. Took claims—the best that was left. While there I met Aleck Carter[4] and the gang who were down on me for trying to hang their pals.

Carter was mounted on a fine, large horse called "Stonewall Jackson." I was afoot. He made a charge to ride over me and tramp me under the horse. He was full of barbwire whisky, but when he saw me go for my six-shooter, he quit. He said: "You grave-digging, scaffold-building s—— of a b——, what are you doing here? Do you want to hang somebody?"

I said I had not yet had the pleasure of digging his grave but hoped to soon see him get there.

My claim proved a failure—having got on a reef of rock. I sunk three or four hundred dollars there and never got an ounce out of it.

Came back to Virginia City, abandoning my claim as also did Steele and others. The people around and in Virginia were at this time in an excited state of mind, and I concluded to quit prospecting for gold and prospect for human fiends.

I got my 8 animals in July, '63, and started for Bannack with a big sack full of gold dust to purchase articles—sugar, etc., that could not be got in Virginia City, that town being literally bought out of provisions. I bought sugar for 60 cents per lb. from Kiscadden, who was a farmer-trader at Denver, and sold it in Virginia for $1.20 per lb. I bought shovels for $14 each and sold them for an ounce. Picks at the same price. I sold gum boots for an ounce an inch—that is, if the foot of the boot was 8 inches long I got 8 ounces of gold for a pair— no matter how long the leg was. But the miners were making

[4] Beidler refers to him variously as "Alec," "Alex," and "Aleck." Thomas J. Dimsdale, in *The Vigilantes of Montana* (Great Falls, 1866; Norman, University of Oklahoma Press, 1953), calls him "Aleck."

money fast and didn't notice it—had to have boots. While at Bannack buying this outfit I run across Buck Stinson and Haze Lyons (the two ducks that had escaped justice and from my graves) at Henry Plummer's gang's headquarters. Buck came up and said: "Your are the ————— that voted to hang me."

I said: "Yes, sir, and if that was the question now, I would still be voting the same way."

Haze Lyons came up and said: "You are the ————— that dug a grave for me."

I said: "Yes, and I never charged you a cent for it."

He said: "I'm not in the grave you dug for me."

I told him he would get there yet—into that same little grave. Buck Stinson was afterwards buried in the grave which I dug for him in Virginia in June, 1863.

All this talk created quite a sensation and drew a large crowd and it was hard to tell which one of the boys it would be at any time. I shook hands with my left hand—with my friends—my right hand was on the navy revolver in my belt. Got my goods packed and lit out from there.

After selling my goods in Virginia I bought a claim in Nevada District with 5 other men—paying $1,600 in dust for it and went to mining and shoveled gravel plenty—worked the claim until late in the fall when we sold out to John Culver for $2,200.

Then the news came up from the Valley that Nick Tbolt[5] was killed and I again went out on the war path. William Herron, who helped search for Tbolt, wrote the following account.

[Herron's account, from an unidentified newspaper clipping:]

During the latter part of November, or the first of December,

[5] Dimsdale, in his *Vigilantes of Montana,* spells this name "Tbalt."

X. Beidler: Vigilante

1863, I was living with my partner, Joseph Bell, in the town of Nevada, following the occupation of a miner. About the first of December, William Clark came from Summit, at the head of Alder Gulch, to our claim and asked me to accompany him to the Stinking Water and help him hunt up Nicholas Tbolt, whom he had sent to John Long's ranch, on the Stinking Water, after a span of mules, stating that he was afraid the road agents had got him. He said that Tbolt had ridden Black Bess,—a mule which I had ridden from California Gulch in Colorado to Alder Gulch. She was an animal that I thought a great deal of, as she had saved my life in Colorado from two Mexican desperadoes, and if there is such a place as a mule heaven I know she got there. She was a splendid saddle animal and the road agents would not hesitate to kill a man to secure her.

Clark also went to X. Beidler and asked him to go along, but X was unable to go and stated as his opinion that Nick had been foully dealt with. I asked Clark to come to the cabin and during dinner we would consider what was best to be done. I had been in his employ nearly two years in Colorado, packing to different mining camps and a portion of the time merchandising. He was a man whom I esteemed very highly, and I could not refuse to accompany him in search of poor Nick, who was ever an honest, upright and faithful man, although I would rather have given $500 than to have gone.

After dinner I prepared myself with a saddle horse and a six-shooter, and proposed to Clark that we should take a couple of shotguns, but he said they would be unnecessary as he had a six-shooter, which he thought was sufficient.

Nothing of importance transpired until we reached Bob Dempsey's ranch, on the Stinking Water, where we dismounted and went in. Clark inquired of Dempsey if he had seen Nick, describing him and telling his errand. Dempsey said he had seen nothing of him, and told us the place where the mules were kept was three or four miles farther down the creek. There were several men and freight teams at Dempsey's and one of the party, a good looking young man well-dressed, stepped up to Clark and said: "Don't you think that Dutchman of yours has skipped to Salt Lake and taken the mules with him?"

Clark's eyes flashed fire (for it was none other than the renowned road agent, George Ives, who had thus accused Nick of being dishonest), and he replied: "That Dutchman is an honest man and some of you damned road agents have killed him and I will avenge him."

Ives started to draw his six-shooter and Clark wasn't any behind him, when Whiskey Bill, one of Ives' confederates, stepped between them and stopped the row. Clark knew they were both road agents and would have shot had I not caught his six-shooter as he drew it.

As we started for Long John's ranch, Ives and Whiskey mounted their horses and went in the same direction. About two and a half miles down the creek the trail followed close to the bank. Clark was riding ahead of me, a few feet in advance, when I noticed something red and called to Clark to stop. On investigation it proved to be a spot of blood about the size of half a dollar. It had snowed, and the wind blowing the snow off the ice, we could discover no tracks that would lead to poor Nick, whose life blood we had seen on the ice, although he lay in the cold embrace of death, not a hundred yards distant.

After remounting, two men rode across our trail, about three hundred yards in advance. I told Clark we had better keep to the right, and out of range of their guns, as Ives and Whiskey Bill had gone to Long John's after their short shot-guns, intending to kill us if we found Nick.

On reaching the ranch Clark went into the wickiup, or Indian tepee, and asked for George Hilderman.[6] A tall gaunt and awkward human being arose from a pile of blankets and shotguns and said: "That is my name."

Clark then told him he was the owner of a span of mules, which he (Hilderman) was working. He [Hilderman] replied that a Dutchman came to get them about a week back; that he was riding a black mule and that the last time seen he was leading the two mules about a half a mile above, at the bend in the creek.

Having learned that Nick got the mules, we started for home, stopping at Dempsey's, where we again met Ives and Whiskey Bill, their horses being hitched and covered with foam, the dreaded shotguns on the pommels of their saddles. Ives asked Clark if he had found his Dutchman yet. Clark replied: "I guess you know where that Dutchman is," but no difficulty occurred.

We then started for Nevada. Reaching Pete Dailey's, Clark proposed to stop for supper. For my part I had seen enough that evening to put me in somewhat of a hurry. I was satisfied that Ives would follow us, and the sight of those guns was not much of an appetizer. Clark carried his point and we dismounted. After hitching the horses, while Clark was ordering supper, I went in and found Clark warming his hands, as unconcerned as if there was no danger whatever. I asked him how long before supper would be ready and he replied: "In a few minutes."

But a short time elapsed when our friends, Ives and Whiskey Bill arrived, carrying the same short shotguns. I thought I had seen those guns often enough for one day, and

[6] In the Beidler manuscript materials, this name is spelled in several different ways. Dimsdale, in his *Vigilantes of Montana*, spells it "Hilderman."

after a lapse of 23 years they are still vividly impressed on my mind. Ives and Bill came into the bar-room and went in to where supper was being prepared. I called Clark outside and told him that those fellows were following us and intended to kill us before we reached Nevada; and finally persuaded him to leave without supper. Clark was not in much of a hurry, neither was I, but I made good use of my spurs, leaving Clark a little in the rear, but continually urging him to keep up. When we reached the point where the Brian's Gulch trail left the road, it was pitch dark. I proposed to take the trail, thinking that our friends would think we took the road on account of the darkness, and thus we would throw them off.

When within a mile of Nevada we felt more secure and slackened our speed. Clark, who had been in California in '49, said: "Those road agents have killed Nick, and I'll tell you what I propose to do. I helped organize the vigilance committee in California and I am going to do the same here, and I will make it hot for them before I die."

The lights of Nevada were now in sight and like the guns, I will never forget them, for they looked as bright as they were welcome that night.

My supposition was correct; Ives and Bill took the road and reached Nevada ahead of us. A few days after someone came to my cabin and told me there was a dead man in a wagon on the street, who had been found on the Stinking Water. On going to see him I recognized him as poor Nick, with a bullet hole in the back of his head. X. Beidler came up and also recognized him, taking a pocket knife from his pocket that he had given him a year previous in Colorado. He had been shot in the head—the two road agents flipping a half dollar to see who should commit the bloody deed, and all.

X. Beidler: Vigilante

Clark was as brave a man as ever breathed; and many a mile he had followed the road agents, through cold and snow, —braving the severest weather, with but a few saddle blankets for a bed and his saddle for a pillow for his old, grey head, in verifying his words to Ives at Dempsey's ranch, that he would avenge Nick's death. God bless him is the prayer of an old-timer, for what he did in ridding the country of the worst gang of cut-throats that ever lived.

The night before Ives was hung, I was in the store where he was being guarded, and bought a can of oysters and asked him to help me eat them. He replied that his appetite was not good. I answered that it was probably as good as mine the night I left Pete Dailey's without my supper.

Wm. Herron

[Beidler's Journal resumes:]

It appears that Tbolt sold a pair of mules to some parties who had paid him the money in advance, and he left to go after the mules and on the way met George Ives who shot him and then robbed him of his money and mules.

Ives accused Long John and a man called the American Pie Eater but both proved themselves innocent. He also accused Aleck Carter of the crime but could not make it stick.

The dead man was not found for about 10 days after he was murdered although we had searched to the best of our ability, and the way we found him, a man by the name of Palmer killed a chicken and it dropped in the willows. His boy went to get the chicken and found it laying upon the body of the dead man.

We brought the body to Nevada. It had been shot through the head and then dragged with a rope to the brush. On searching the pockets of the victim we found a knife which Tom Baume[7] had loaned him in my presence.

A party was organized to capture Ives and left Nevada in the night. He along with Long John and Tex were arrested and on the way back, George Ives made a break for liberty by starting his horse on a dead run and he came mighty near getting away. It took about 3 hours to recapture him and he would have been hung on the spot, only the guards wanted to show the people that he could be brought in alive.

The news of the capture was soon known all along the Gulch.

[7] Beidler sometimes spells this name "Baum."

[IV]

The Story of George Ives

BY COL. WILBUR FISK SANDERS

GEORGE IVES, according to current information, was born at Ives' Grove, Racine County, Wisconsin, where, at the time of his death, he had a widowed mother and some sisters living. The circumstances of his later life were such, that, as is usual in such cases, little can be ascertained of his history.

In the late '50's he was in Oregon, in charge of pack trains, for the United States army, under Gen. Wright, and possibly Col. Steptoe. He was a young man of splendid physique and attractive personal appearance, of indomitable will and a rugged constitution; an accomplished marksman, a bold rider, resourceful, generous, and brave; a favorite among the officers and men, and other persons with whom he came in contact. It is said that he here became cognizant of a band of freebooters who infested Oregon, lying in wait for treasure, which in these early days had been discovered and then extracted in small quantities at various points in British Columbia, and what was then central Oregon, and which nevertheless amounted in the aggregate to tempting quantities of gold dust, which accumulated upon the trails leading from the mining camps toward Portland, then the principal seaport of the Northwest, and the point of departure by river and sea to California. It has been said of Ives, and it is not improbable, that in some instances, knowing the point of danger from these robbers, he warned the owners of this gold dust, who were his friends, of their presence, and enabled them to save their earnings. However this may be, nothing current as to his Oregon history is to his discredit.

He left the employ of the Government officers, and early came to the eastern frontier of Oregon. We hear of him at Lewiston, Pierce City, Elk City, Florence diggings, and Warren's diggings. Already there were substantial discoveries of placer mines in eastern Idaho, or what is now Montana. How his life was spent during this period, or who were his companions has not appeared. Alex Carter, another character of some interest to the early pioneers of Montana, seems to have been one of his companions, and if the few rumors then extant concerning him be true, in his activities and qualities he much resembled Ives, although the latter had a personal magnetism which Carter did not possess.

There was a small Mormon settlement at Fort Lenhi, on the head waters of the Salmon River, which derived its principal consequence from its isolation, and as being the abode of divers and sundry recalcitrant Mormons, known as "Josephites," who, dissenting from the authorities of the Church at "The State of Deseret" around Salt Lake, and being disturbed by the hostilities between the Mormon Church and the Government of the United States, had withdrawn themselves from the turmoil around that inland sea and had occupied, among some poverty stricken and spiritless Indians, their peaceful valley. This settlement misled many travellers, prospectors, adventurers and engineers, who thought that from thence it were an easy task to follow down the Salmon Riven to its junction with the Snake or Lewis River; an effort in which, by reason of rocky cañons, impenetrable forests and impassible water-falls, and to which, in the early '70's engineers of the Northern Pacific Railroad Company had been compelled to surrender. It required seven-

41

ty years of exploration to finally ascertain that this route was wholly impracticable.

Ives came to eastern Idaho, as the Beaverhead country was then called, in 1862, lured thither by the report of rich gold discoveries on the Grasshopper, and on Gold Creek or "American Fork," as Gold Creek was then designated. Enough rumors of gold having been found on the head waters of streams in the Rocky Mountains had been floating around in common speech for some years to give credence to the report that it had been found in large quantities, and to make the exaggerations of the richness of these placers easy of belief, and although the earliest discoveries were neither vast nor rich, as gold discoveries are usually supposed to be, they obtained an early repute in both respects beyond what the facts would justify, and as the reports spread by means of casual and irregular messengers, the stories grew in proportion to the distance they were carried, they created the dominant excitement, where it was a world of excitement, among the few travellers over a radius of five hundred miles or more. Happily, as prospectors, adventurers, miners, and speculators came, the actual discoveries in richness and area grew apace, so that there was no disappointment, although many disgruntled adventurers, after a brief survey of some of the richest placer mines the world has ever known, retired in disgust, declaring them to be of no value. This was true in instances of Alder Gulch, in the Beaverhead country, one of the richest mines of placer gold probably in the world.

Although the discovery of gold at the Grasshopper was subsequent to that at Gold Creek, its superior richness, and easy working, coupled with the greater pertinacity of the discoverers and miners there, created the little hamlet of "East Bannack," and made it the centre of interest during the winter of 1862–3. There were other points in this region where discoveries of gold in limited quantities were made, but Bannack City held the centre of the stage until June 1863, when it was compelled to surrender to the extensive discoveries on Alder Creek seventy miles east.

Food was somewhat scarce throughout this entire region, as so large an advent of denizens had not been expected, the limited supplies of Fort Benton were early exhausted, and long drafts were required to be made from the Danes and Yankees of Salt Lake Valley, and the Missourians, who had demonstrated already the fertility of the valley of the Walla Walla. There would have been some suffering at various camps in this Beaverhead country, had there not been a profusion of game. It everywhere abounded. If in the winter some of it became poor, it was nevertheless healthy, and it sustained in reasonable comfort, supplemented by a little flour, dried fruit, and bacon imported from more distant regions, some 500 to 1,000 people. Whiskey, tea, coffee, sugar, salt, and tobacco were esteemed as luxuries to be moderately enjoyed, if obtainable, or to be omitted in the *cuisine* if not to be had. The Indians looked upon the influx of the miners with a sullen disapproval, some of the small settlements were practically besieged, and it was not safe for men to travel through the valleys and over the mountains except in companies, and then only with the utmost watchfulness. Men scampered over valley and mountain from camp to camp, now dodging war parties of Indians, or joining other travellers for mutual protection, and withal their watchfulness experiencing narrow escapes, or bloody tragedies.

A growing conviction, justified by observation, that the country was rich in gold, gave an air of hopeful cheerfulness to the denizens of these wilds, and made their ambition and their courage virtues.

George Ives' advent into these mining camps was a circumstance which added to intercommunication, for he was tireless, well mounted, without a local habitation, sociable, and took an interest in what was happening around him. For some years he had spent his life in the midst of Indian hostilities, and while he did not hold them in disdain, he was full of strategy, and had confidence in his own resources, which had been justified by many narrow escapes. He met in these early settlements, a number of men, who, in other regions, had established a firm repute as criminals, and who had escaped from the justice, the laws of which they had violated. Reputations like these had a wide circulation, and it was not long before those who bore them recognized each other, and were drawn together by mutual experiences and vices. As the best security against punishment for crime, some of them aspired to seize upon the efficient instrumentalities of justice, but Ives seems to have been content to let political affairs alone, if so be he could be a free rider along the valleys, through cañon, mountain, and plain. In the early summer of 1863 he spent sometime in the Snake River Valley, along the roads leading to Boise and the Beaverhead country, where, in the vicinity of Market Lake he paid a visit to a little party on its way to Bannack, of which I was one.

The horses in use in this region were cayuses or Indian ponies, small of stature, patient of toil, inured to the food and life to which they were compelled, and of great endurance. There were some Bronchos or California horses, a little larger in size, tougher in constitution, and uglier in temper, who bore the brands of their Southern owners. Rarer than these was the tall rangy American horse, agile, masterful and swift of foot, coveted by equestrians, and wherever it appeared, drawing interest and undivided attention. Ives was the possessor of such an one, and he sat his saddle like a swan on a billowy lake. He had plenty of money. Upon his visit to our camp near Market Lake, he had shown to us a sack of gold dust containing nuggets, the first we had ever seen, and which seemed to our inexperienced eyes, phenomenal productions of Nature. Having been so long in the vicinity of the frontier, he was well posted as to those enterprises and industries which insured profit, and as it was necessary he should have an ostensible vocation, he established, on Daylight Creek in Alder Gulch, a corral for the care of the horses and cattle of wayfarers, whose interests required them to remain in that vicinity for a greater or lesser period. Teams were continually arriving at this commercial centre of Alder Gulch; sometimes a single span of horses, sometimes great trains of 26 wagons, drawn by two or three spans of horses or mules. The entire country was covered with nutritious and waving grasses, growing higher than any present observation would indicate. He secured by a claim a ranch for the "night herd" at the head of Daylight Gulch, and upon the divide toward the Madison River, and some 22 miles below Virginia City, near Wisconsin Creek, he found ample pasturage for another and larger band of horses, where he kept his "day herd." Tents furnished sufficient accommodation for his herders, who with greater or lesser fidelity looked after his stock. His business was somewhat extensive, but it did not monopolize his time, which was spent in riding, robbery, and revelry. Sudden and swift in quarrel if thereto provoked, he was, when sober, sociable, generous, peaceable, and there was not much of the braggart about him. When he was drunk, it was difficult to get along with him, all the demons of passion seemed to be let loose within him. He was of the aristocracy of the Corsairs, and men of lesser courage, wickedness, and resources, gathered about him as to a magnet.

He did not have the prudence or wiles of Plummer, nor did he act with Plummer's cool and calculating strategy, but he supplemented that remarkable character in a very evident degree. While Plummer maintained his headquarters at Bannack, which was the gate-way out of the country, Ives was circulating through all the multiplying camps in the region, keeping track of mining production, and the larger commercial enterprises, so that he knew where the accumulations of gold dust were liable to be, and when they would probably be carried from the country. No horseman, pack train, or ox teams or other trains left the region that Plummer, Ives, and Gallagher and a dozen others did not know whether they transported gold dust in quantities, and this information was a common possession. Along the ways of exit from the country they maintained "look-outs" and many a miner bit the dust because of his known personal successes, or because he was entrusted with the treasure belonging to his acquaintances. More than one hundred instances of these homicides were inventoried by the early settlers.

The story became a monotonous one. The contempt of human life became a growing quality, and murders within the limits of the settlements became of increasing frequency. Pretexts for these of greater or lesser plausibility were made, but the taste for blood grew upon that on which it fed. Sometimes an aroused volatile indignation refused to accept these pretences, and demanded a more thorough investigation, when Plummer, the great minister of order, would proceed to the investigation, and the affair would be closed, sometimes by suppressing investigations, and sometimes by a trial organized to acquit.

Late in the summer of 1863 it began to dawn upon the Virginia City citizens that these highway robbers were plying their vocation with great industry, but as they dominated the executive officers of the volunteer tribunals the mouths of the suspicious were sealed. With increasing certainty, and ever-widening scope, this open secret, at first a suspicion grew into an absolute certainty, told in whispers, and strangers in the country who had gained each other's confidence began to consult as to the protection of their enterprises and themselves, and even dared to speak confidentially the names of the guilty parties.

Plummer's prudent reticence delayed suspicion as to him longer than some of the others, and quite a number of the robbers were known before Plummer was suspected. He was a candidate for United States Marshal of the new territory with respectable but limited support. He was able to render his subordinate good service by misleading public opinion and misdirecting this suspicion, but by the autumn of 1863, public fame, informed by a multitude of circumstances, pointing her unerring finger at as bloody a company of bandits as ever rode the plains.

In the summer of 1863 Messrs. Clark and Burtchey came to Alder Gulch from Colorado, and locating at Summit, engaged in various industrial enterprises at that place. Not having use for all their teams, and esteeming highly a large span of mules, which had arrived at the end of its long journey in an exhausted condition, Mr. Clark had turned them over to Ives that they might recuperate at his ranch, on Wisconsin Creek, where they remained for a considerable period of time. Having occasion to use them early in December, he sent a young man after them. This young man was a German, who, accompanying his parents up the Platte, had been left an orphan by the Indians, who had killed his father and mother. He was living with, and probably adopted by Henry Clark, with whom he was a great favorite. His absence after the mules was greatly prolonged, when about the middle of December, his mutilated body in a light freight wagon, covered by a blanket, was drawn up Alder Gulch to Virginia

City, in charge of one William A. Palmer, the keeper of a saloon and dance-house at Nevada City. Mr. Palmer, a few days before, had gone to Wisconsin Creek and its vicinity on a hunting expedition, and shooting a bird upon the wing, he discovered a dead body near where his game had fallen. It was a gruesome sight, having already suffered from birds and beasts of prey, and he was greatly disturbed at his find. Seeing the tents of Ives' headquarters not far distant, he endeavored to secure assistance from their occupants to load the body into his wagon, that he might convey it to Virginia City for burial, but he was met with rebuff, and expressions of some surprise that he should concern himself so much at a circumstance which, he was assured, was one of frequent occurrence, happening indeed, almost every day. Nothing daunted, however, he rolled the frozen body into a blanket, lifted it into his wagon, and returned to Virginia City, making frequent stoppages in the Gulch for such consolation as would strengthen his courage, and relating the circumstances of his discovery. A more than usual interest was excited in the homicide, which was heightened by the mutilated form of the boy, which for purposes of identification was frequently examined by the citizens along the Gulch. There was no wagon road from Virginia City to Summit, although over the hill, as far up as Highland, there was a timber road, and I think the body of Tbolt, enclosed in a pine box, was packed on the back of a burro to Summit and buried. Of this, however, I do not feel sure.

In one or two days thereafter, a mounted party from Summit reached Virginia City in the afternoon, where they were joined by some citizens, and it was reported that their errand was the arrest of the murderers of the young man, if they could be ascertained. Of this party were Henry Clark, George Burtchey, Elkanah Morse, Nelson or Elias Story, H. K.

Harvey and one or two others from Summit, and they were joined at Virginia City by J. X. Beidler, Thos. Baume, Frank Angevine, and some others, and wended their way down the Gulch. They proceeded to the point where the body had been found, and at early dawn the next morning swooped down upon the tents which constituted Ives' ranch, and awakened five or six sleepers somewhat suddenly, all of whom were arrested. Taking charge of their arms, they proceeded to examine the prisoners separate and apart, and ascertaining that two or three of them were mere wayfarers stopping over night, without identification with the location, they detained only George Ives, George Hillerman, (known in the slang of the day as "The Great American Pie-Biter"), a man advanced in years, without much dominant force or intellectual possession, and John Frank,[1] known by the soubriquet of "Long John." Ives proffered them a breakfast, of which they partook, and bringing in from the herd horses for the prisoners, they saddled up, and started for Alder Gulch.

It was three or four miles to Dempsey's Bridge, across the Stinking Water River, which at that time was a prominent point, where the robbers had established a look-out, and kept a picket, who advised them of the coming and going of travellers on the Bannack road. Jimmy Gibbings, a young boy, discharged most of this duty. On the way up the river Ives boasted of the speed of his horse, and challenged the party to a race, and came near making his escape by that ruse.

I have no desire to inventory Ives' crimes. During the summer he had spent some time in the Snake River valley with every insignia of a highway robber, at points where highway robberies and murders were frequent, introducing himself to strangers or being introduced by companions as "Judge Lewis from the upper country," the Hon. E. P. Lewis, formerly of

[1] Dimsdale, in *The Vigilantes of Montana,* spells this name "Franck."

Sumner, in Kansas, being an excellent and popular citizen in this region. There was no definite proof, however, of Ives' complicity with these early robberies and murders, nor could they be traced to any particular person.

In the late summer he returned to the Beaverhead country, and although frequently at Bannack, Virginia City and other settlements, his headquarters were in the saddle. Two or three vagabond herders and a manager being sufficient to conduct his business, gave him leisure to pursue his inclinations as he chose. He was drunk in the towns with increasing frequency, and he used to ride to the doors of the mercantile establishments and borrow money with great informality, and without consulting deferentially the desires of the merchants to make the loan, omitting also any suggestion as to when it would be returned. However, in many instances, the gold dust so obtained was repaid.

It was his favorite habit at this time, dismounting at the door of a saloon or store, to enter the house leading his horse in with him, and departing when his visit was concluded.

Late in November, as I was starting from Bannack to Virginia City, Henry Plummer asked if I knew Ives, and telling him that I did, he handed me a letter addressed to him, with a request that I deliver it when I should see him. The morning after my arrival in Virginia City I saw Ives on his horse in front of the store where I made my headquarters, and I handed him Plummer's letter, and returned to the table in the building where I did my work. In a few minutes Ives entered the door, leading his horse to the back part of the store, where I was sitting, and thrust into my hand Plummer's letter, with a request that I read it. I disclaimed any interest or curiosity as to its contents, but he insisted that I read it and I did so. It contained a statement that Plummer had met Ives' partner at Bannack who had inquired as to his location, saying that he wished to start the next week for Salt Lake City, and desired Ives to come and settle and divide the partnership property, and saying he thought he should come at once. I returned the letter to Ives without further thought as to the significance of its contents, and it has been left to my imagination since that time to wonder what it portended.

On the 18th day of December I was at Nevada City, having a final interview with a gentleman who had taken an interest in endeavoring to secure the creation and organization of a new territory in eastern Idaho, and was about to return to Virginia City, whence the next morning I was to go to Bannack, my home, and where I anticipated spending my first Christmas in the mountains, when my attention was attracted to a cavalcade of horsemen coming up the main street. As they approached I recognized them as the gentlemen who had gone down the Gulch the day before to detect and arrest, if possible, Tbolt's murderers, with four or five additional persons.

Twilight had already come, and they stopped without dismounting in the middle of the road and continued a discussion as to whether they would take the prisoners to Virginia City, or remain with them at Nevada. From the trend of their observations it was apparent this had been the subject of some previous consideration. There were those who thought it was due to the prisoners that they should have the selection of the forum of their trial, and Ives expressed an earnest desire to be conducted to Virginia City, where he said he had "friends." Others were of the opinion that deference to established custom required that the prisoners, without regard to the mere desire of any one of them should be tried by some substantial tribunal nearest the scene of the tragedy,—a vague recognition of the value of the Anglo-Saxon doctrine of the jury of the vicinage. Upon putting the question to the vote the prisoners and Jimmy Gibbings assumed to vote, and the question seemed to be in danger of becoming a tie, when someone insisted that it was a question upon which none should vote but those who had made the arrest, and had charge of the prisoners, and so it was determined that they should be tried in Nevada mining district, which was nearest to Ives' ranch, with the insignificant exception of Junction Mining District, then in a chrysalis and fickle state, having been recently organized. The prisoners were taken to a small warehouse on the main street which seemed to offer reasonable security and accommodation, their blankets and robes given them, a guard appointed, and the crowd dispersed.

On my way up to Virginia City, I met a lawyer of prominence and ability hastening down to Nevada, who advised me that some of his clients were in trouble, having been accused and arrested for the murder of the "Dutchman." He said he was counsel for "these fellows," whoever he may have meant thereby. This lawyer was James M. Thurmond, who asked me to return with him, stating there was an opportunity for me to make a good fee, as they had plenty of money. I proceeded towards Virginia City, and shortly met another lawyer, John D. Ritchie, one of the earliest practitioners in this region, who was considered essential to the winning of cases, whether before mining judges, or juries on miners' meetings. He was already far gone with consumption, against which he made a stout fight for a number of years, finally dying at Missoula.

Arriving at the foot of Wallace Street in Virginia City, I saw Harry Percival Adams Smith, another lawyer, who, though somewhat demoralized, was a man of very remarkable ability. He was fortifying himself at the last place of entertainment, for his journey to Nevada, and advised me that he had been sent for to help some of "the boys" out of a scrape. These three lawyers were somewhat remarkable characters, all of them out to thwart the administration of justice by all the means they could invent.

The next morning, in the store of D. W. Tilton & Co., where A. J. Oliver & Co. kept their express office, which assumed largely the business of a stage and postoffice, I was purchasing my ticket for a passage to Bannack, when I was accosted by A. J. Culbertson, with the statement that the Lott Brothers wished to see me at once at Nevada. I told him I was going through Nevada on the stage in the course of a couple of hours, and would take occasion to see them as I passed through. He stated to me, however, that there was much urgency in their desire, and that he thought I should go to them at once without waiting for the coach or purchasing my ticket, and I accompanied him forthwith to Nevada.

Arriving there I was advised by these gentlemen that the lawyers then practicing in Alder Gulch had all been engaged, so far as they could ascertain, to defend the murderers of Tbolt; that the testimony which had been secured demonstrated that the guilty parties had been arrested; that it had been a most cruel murder, and they greatly desired that I should remain to prosecute the defendants. I had not been present at any trial for homicide in the mountain region, but my ears had been filled with stories of the provoking miscarriages of justice with a single exception, arising largely from the disinclination of participants to accept the responsibilities which their position imposed. The courts would disclaim responsibility as to the facts of any murder, and lawyers would tell the jury that if the defendant was guilty he should be convicted, but if they entertained a reasonable doubt he should be acquitted; that the jurymen were the judges of the fact, and that they must do what they thought was right, etc. The lawyers disclaimed any inclination to argue upon one

53

side or the other as to the guilt or innocence of the parties accused. Of course, the preliminary motion to quash the proceedings, to defer the trial, to continue the case, to delay the matter until the sense of offended justice had somewhat died out of the community; till opportunity had been afforded to ascertain who were the witnesses; to scatter or manipulate them by such persuasions as they were susceptible to, were as well known then as now, and were practiced with unfailing uniformity. I had made up my mind in the light of all this history and from my knowledge of human nature, as it appeared in the administration of criminal law, that if I should prosecute any case, I would push it with the utmost vigor, and if the guilt of the accused was certain, that the retribution should be swift, and absolutely remorseless. This was essential in defence of every person who took a responsible and active part in the prosecution, and it was a matter also of personal self-defence. The surroundings did not wholly prophesy the character of this prosecution, nor all that transpired, but I accepted the position.

Having gathered from the members of the *posse* the story of the killing of Tbolt, as they had ascertained it from John Frank and others, I interviewed him and Palmer, who had discovered the body, and found them apparently willing to testify. The citizens of Nevada and miners from up and down the Gulch had assembled in considerable numbers before noon upon a mining claim between the Main Street of Nevada and Alder Creek, and I went there, practically an unknown person, to find a meeting presided over by Hon. Don L. Byam, and the lawyers and miners considering the code of criminal procedure to be observed in the trial of this particular case. In the absence of the defendants, their lawyers were desirous that the trial should be in the regular form, before a miner's judge and a jury of six or twelve men selected in the usual way, but it had already been voted that the trial should take place before the miners of the Gulch en masse, to be presided over by Judge Byam, with the assistance of the judge of Junction Mining District below Nevada, who fulfilled the office of *puisne* judge, and a motion was made that lawyers should not be permitted to participate in the trial. This question begot a heated discussion, in which Messrs. Thurmond, Ritchie, and Smith took an important part, and with Col. J. M. Wood, and some other citizens, advocating the right of the parties to be represented by counsel. The proposition, however, was vehemently, if not stoutly, opposed by a great many orators present from the sluice-boxes and the unfortunate lawyers suffered much depreciation, and excoriation. The discussion lasted for an hour or more, and one of the participants, most loud-mouthed and censorious in his denunciation of the profession, was the owner of a mine at the mouth of Brown's Gulch, who had recently belonged to a Detroit regiment in the Federal army, and who upon this occasion wore his uniform. It may seem laughable or even trifling, but watching the drift and current of speech on that occasion, I do not doubt but that his uniform lost him his case.

After the discussion had been unduly prolonged, someone suggested that they would like to hear my opinion as to the advisability of permitting lawyers to participate, and in response to the invitation I mounted the wagon, and looked out upon the somewhat heterogeneous crowd, with a few exceptions being to me entire strangers. I was conscious that I was subjected to a somewhat inquisitive inspection, for the lawyers who represented the defendants to that moment were the leaders of the Bar, and represented its intellect and influence in the various controversies appealing to courts and masses for determination. There had been added that morning to the trio I have already mentioned, Alexander Davis, Esq., a most

55

excellent and pertinacious gentleman, who was a substantial addition in more ways than one to the defendant's strength.

There were, indeed, three or four other lawyers in the Gulch, who subsequently practised their profession, but they had not yet assumed to practise law there, or were such recent arrivals as that their capacity had not become known. I did not think it desirable to appear as taking a great interest in the question of permitting counsel, although my own conviction was, that if the defendants desired lawyers to defend them it should, under all circumstances, be granted. I said to the crowd that in determining a question of that character they should have regard to the final result, that if the parties should be tried and convicted or acquitted, whether they would be more satisfied with the result according as they had granted or refused them the privilege of being heard by counsel, and that I thought they should consider the matter seriously in that light. I mentioned casually that I had been spoken to by friends of the party who had been killed to prosecute the case, if lawyers were permitted to participate, and that I trusted we should be able in that case to come at the truth of the matter, and protect all the interests confided to our care.

The crowd looked at me curiously as if taking the measure of my ability to cope with the great lawyers of established reputation who were on the other side, and they did not give any sign of satisfaction with the condition. However, on putting the question to the vote, our ex-federal soldier was beaten, and it was determined that the defendants should have the benefit of counsel, if benefit it were.

It was late in December, and the weather was somewhat cold. It was very evident that the men who were to try the defendants, would not, all of them, hear all the testimony, and therefore upon my motion it was resolved that they should be separately tried, and that as to Ives, who was universally recognized as the principal culprit, we should have from each of the mining districts twelve jurymen, making twenty-four in all, whose duty it should be to listen to all the proof, and give such advice to the meeting as justly resulted therefrom. Whereupon Judge Byam wrote the names of twelve miners, Judge Wilson the names of twelve others, and it was moved that these twenty-four should constitute the jurors in the case whose duties were advisory merely.

The excitement of the crowd meanwhile had greatly increased. From eight to ten miles up the gulch, and two to three miles below, the miners, with their guns, were arriving in great numbers, until a thousand or fifteen hundred had assembled around that wagon. At this stage of the proceedings Mr. J. B. Cavan, a bailiff or deputy sheriff of Henry Plummer's, mounted the wagon and read a list of twelve names of citizens of Fairweather Mining District, whom he moved should be added to the twenty-four already selected. I thought the jury somewhat clumsy by reason of its number, and I objected to adding the list of Mr. Cavan thereto, saying that it appertained to the organized mining districts with a chosen judicial autonomy to try the defendants, which were nearest the scene of the crime; that we had included Nevada mining district by reason of the incompleteness and smallness of the organization at Junction, and that I did not think it wise to enlarge it by going yet further up the Gulch, and that no reason could be given, if we did proceed further, why Highland Mining District, and Pine Grove, and Summit might not also claim the privilege of increasing the number of the jury.

The deliberations of the forenoon, and the vote upon the proposition to allow Ives the privilege of counsel, not only gave confidence to the lawyers, but it emboldened his chums, allies, and sympathizers in the crowd, who took a very active part in the proceedings, and in the applause, which became somewhat frequent, and it was apparent that a fight was on of very great strenuousness. The "good fellows," the popular fellows, the generous fellows, the well-known fellows, in short, the boys, without care or knowledge of Ives' guilt or innocence, led by a half-dozen active colleagues of Ives, had interested themselves in the controversy, and made that interest manifest by encouragement or interruptions with great freedom. When I had finished what I had to say against adding to the twenty-four jurors another list of twelve from the district above, Mr. Cavan vehemently shook a paper containing this list of names in my face, and before the assembled miners said, "Perhaps you have something to say against the character of these men I have named." As a matter of fact I did not know one of them, but as he had read the list I recognized the name of a prominent gambler at Virginia City, with whom I subsequently became acquainted, and feeling bound to maintain the rights of the prosecution there, I replied that I had nothing to say against the list of names, that I did not know one of them, and that if what I heard with reference to some of them was true, I had no desire to make their acquaintance. This excited his anger to a somewhat intemperate degree, and standing by my side, speaking to me for the benefit of the crowd, he said, "I will hold you personally responsible for that remark,"—and the whole tumult of the Ives' trial arose that moment. In that strange and new country it would not do to treat a remark of that kind with indifference, nor the speaker without some personal attention, and in language as pregnant with meaning as I could select, I gave him a verbal castigation in the presence of that crowd which permitted no misunderstanding as to its significance. I said I was busy in a matter which occupied my time, that I did not fail to apprehend the meaning of his remark when used by gentlemen, that evidently he had indulged in that speech to advertise a courage which he did not possess, that I was reasonably certain that he was a coward, but that at the close of the trial I should be in the vicinity, and could be found. This little colloquy stirred the miners profoundly, and by their cheers they seemed to think he got no more than he deserved, and they looked at me with increasing interest, and apparent confidence.

I think it just to Mr. Cavan to say that a subsequent acquaintance with him, and a knowledge of his career for some years thereafter dissipated any supposition that his action resulted from any sympathy with highway robbery and murder, or any desire to shield and protect the guilty, but that it was a move by him which he thought would be popular and make him friends.

It was now noon, and Judge Byam declared the meeting adjourned till after dinner. Robert Hereford was Judge Byam's executive officer in his position as sheriff of Nevada Mining District, and Adriel B. Davis the sheriff of Junction Mining District acted as Hereford's deputy. At this time Judge Wilson approached me, and inquired if I desired assistance in the prosecution, and oppressed somewhat with the growing consequence of the battle, I cheerfully said I did. He said there was a lawyer who was mining at Junction, who he thought could render valuable help, and I asked him to introduce me to him. He brought to me a short, stubby, hairy, fatherly-looking man, somewhat rude, of dilapidated garb, whose bootlegs did not have sufficient fibre to stand up, and into one of which he had vainly essayed to tuck one of the legs of his pantaloons. He spoke intelligently, and made it manifest that his indignation was deeply stirred by the events which had transpired, and I counted it fortunate that on all accounts such a find had been made. His name was Charles S. Bagg, and I found no occasion to regret his identification with the prosecution. If the lawyers for the defence appealed to the miners on questions submitted, the appeal of my colleague was with greater frequency and intensity to the Almighty, with whom, judging from his speech, he was on terms of considerable intimacy. He lacked nothing of audacity and volubility, and being himself a miner, he appealed to the assemblage on their level with great effect, his courage was equal to the duty, and he rendered good service throughout the trial.

After dinner the scene of the event was changed from the mining claim where the morning session had been held to the east side of the main street in Nevada, where a big Schuttler wagon had been drawn up in front of a two story building, some seats arranged for the Court, counsel, and prisoners in the same, and a fire had been built on the ground near the wagon from cord wood which some unlucky woodman had the misfortune to have placed in that vicinity. William Y. Pemberton, Esq., then a genial young lawyer living at Virginia City, was appointed amanuensis and a table was provided for him near the fire. A semi-circle of benches from an adjacent hurdy-gurdy house had been placed round the fire for the accommodation of the twenty-four jurors, and behind that semi-circle a place was reserved for a cordon of guards, who with their shotguns or rifles as the case might be, marched hour by hour. Beyond them, and round on their flank stood a thousand or fifteen hundred miners, teamsters, mechanics, merchants, gamblers, all sorts and conditions of men, deeply interested in the proceedings. As a rule, it was a good-natured crowd and not unduly boisterous, and all had the right of participating in the discussions and other proceedings if they chose, of which quite a number from time to time availed themselves. There was frequent objection to the relevancy or pertinency of proposed proof, and whenever a proposition was submitted to a vote, the absent participants were summoned from the restaurants, saloons, stores, barber shops, and other places of resort to give their vote upon the objections, which was generally without merit, and were overruled.

While it was cold, there was very little suffering, and during the middle part of the day the sun, which swung lazily round the southern horizon, gave some warmth. The miners were generally warmly dressed, and did not make any complaints, nor abandon in the least degree the purpose for which they had come to the trial. Another freight wagon with a very high seat had been conveniently placed for the accommodation of the witness who was testifying, in view of all the persons present. The first witness was Palmer, who, mounting the high seat above the entire crowd presented a somewhat uncouth appearance, as with bared head, and long hair hanging upon his shoulders, he told the story of his acquaintance with Ives, his finding of the dead body, his application for assistance in loading it into his wagon, and the declination thereof. This story he told in a loud and confident voice with perfect freedom, and apparent willingness, and his manner seemed to give confidence to the subsequent witnesses. Expectation stood on tip-toe as to what the proof would be, for rumor asserted that some one had turned State's evidence, if that is a name to apply where it was a thousand miles to a State.

From the opening of the trial new facts began to come to the ears of the prosecution, told generally in whispers, with a request that the name of the person imparting the information might be withheld, or in some instances that it might be made to appear that the information was compulsorily extorted. The afternoon of the 19th of December saw the trial fairly under way. The miners adjourned till 9 o'clock the next morning, and the prisoners were remanded to the warehouse under guard.

There was no lull in the excitement, while rumors came from every point of the compass, prophesying dire disaster to the prosecution or defence, according to the inclination of the prophet or liar who invented them. Detectives and pickets were detailed to watch events during the preliminary proceedings, and for the first day or two of the trial "Alec" Carter and "Doc" Hunter, with a half dozen other friends of Ives who were believed to be identified with him in his crimes, had been very active in his behalf, insisting upon whatever, in their judgment, would insure his acquittal. Plummer, the acknowledged civic magnate of that Gulch and the entire country, and the elected sheriff, under the mining regulations of two districts remote from each other, was a name to conjure with an object of great interest, and rumor affirmed that he was on his way from Bannack to take the prisoners from the possession of the party who had them in charge and on trial. As a matter of actual fact, when the prisoners had been brought to Nevada, by the advice of their counsel George Lane, brutally nicknamed "Club-foot George," had been dispatched in the night to Bannack for Plummer's presence and assistance. But there were rumors circulating in Bannack which disturbed the confidence of Plummer and illustrated that "uneasy lies the head that wears a crown." It was said there that there had been formed in Alder Gulch a great vigilance committee intent on ridding the country of the lawful authorities, and divers and sundry good citizens besides, whose names were given with a view to add to the obloquy of such a movement. These rumors found credence with Plummer, and with other good citizens of Bannack, and a picket post was established on the top of the mountain divide, between the Grasshopper and Rattlesnake, to watch the approach of such a party so all the importunings of Plummer to go to the rescue were declined.

Ives was primarily accused and tried for murder, and in tracing his whereabouts for the summer and fall preceding, circumstances of robbery and murder thickened around him, and the names of his companions on these forays were blurted out by witnesses with a brutal frankness, and the testimony assumed a wider scope than the mere proof of killing Tbolt. As the names of these active participants, in the earlier portion of the proceedings were frequently repeated, under circumstances showing their identification with Ives' crimes, a prudent regard for their own safety silenced them, and retiring to the rear of the trial some of them disappeared. Of course, such an assemblage was a motley crowd, made up as it was of all classes of people inhabiting the Gulch. Generally it may be said they were sober, industrious, adventurous, hard-working miners, with a clear conception of their right to be, to do, to have and to keep; with a strong sense of justice, born, not of studying the definition in the books, but of that experience derivable from contact with the world and its affairs. Merchants and freighters, mechanics and teamster, equally sober and impelled by like convictions, constituted a limited fraction of the crowd.

One of the active participants in the discussion was a man from Georgia, Col. John M. Wood, who divided his time between mining, speculating, carousing and preaching the Gospel to congregations yet ruder than he. His motive in mingling actively in this trial was probably a desire to introduce himself to the community and establish his character as a man of some consequence, for with all his activity it is not probable that he had any sympathy with the crimes then frequent. He had come from Colorado, and what though he clung to his Baptist religion with great vigor, he had a wild latitudinarianism which rendered it very uncertain on which side of any controversy impinging on morals he would be found. In the various discussions in which he took part, he was uniformly found, for reasons which he plausibly dressed, on the side of the culprits, until the crowd, which through all the proceedings maintained an imperturbable good nature, occasionally jeered him. I am sorry I cannot name all of the miners and others who participated in these discussions, which prolonged the trial unnecessarily, but it was thought advisable to give the amplest latitude to discussion, and an equal freedom to decision.

The testimony of John Frank, given freely and with apparent candor, told the circumstances of the killing of Tbolt. Tbolt had appeared at Ives' ranch or headquarters, presented the order of Mr. Clark for the mules, and they had been brought up and delivered to him. They were large, and very valuable, and feeding on the nutritious grass had become silky and high-spirited. When Tbolt came to settle the bill, his buckskin purse, out of which the dust was weighed, contained three or four hundred dollars. Mounting one of the mules, he started across the valley toward the highway leading to Alder Gulch. After he had departed Ives suggested that it was a pity to let all that money go and the mules also, and when, by the toss of a gold coin, the lot fell to him to prevent it, he saddled his horse, examined his revolver, and galloped after his victim. Returning with the mules in a short time, in a spirit of explanation or bravado, he said that it seemed cowardly to shoot a fellow in the back, and when he approached near enough, he holloaed, and when Tbolt turned round, he made a centre shot, hitting him in the head. He took the purse, and drove the mules back to camp.

The stage drivers upon the line from Virginia City and

Bannack, regular and occasional, gave much information as to Ives' connection with robberies and murders occurring along that highway, and of persons who were cognizant of the same, but it was thought prudent to excuse them from testifying, because of their necessary exposure to the vengeance of Ives and his partners in crime, but the proof of the killing of Tbolt, of the fact that Ives had been engaged in coach robberies, had perpetrated other murders, and had spent weeks along the line of exit out of the country where treasure was carried was ample and absolutely conclusive. The foolish attempt by some of his partners in crime to establish an alibi as to some of these crimes broke down ignominiously, and it became very apparent to his counsel on the second day of the trial that if he were to be acquitted or otherwise escape, it must be for something other than the result of the proof, and with great ingenuity they sought to bring the prosecution into contempt, and excite the prejudices of the crowd against it. Long John, who had turned State's evidence, and related the circumstances of the main tragedy with great distinctness, and who had been corroborated by many circumstances relevant and irrelevant, came in for the seven vials of the lawyers' wrath. They dwelt, with great fervor and indignation upon the infamy manifested by a participant in crime who would "peach on his pals," and argued that whatever might be said as to the actual perpetrator of the crime, the traitor should never be permitted to escape. A code of morals sounding very much like this re-appeared in Montana a generation later. Before Ives' case was disposed of, his several lawyers seemed to think they had firmly established the proposition that whatever was the result as to Ives, Long John should certainly be executed.

The great excitement culminated upon the last day of the trial which was almost wholly devoted to the arguments of the case. The proximity of two hostile armies would not have been more productive of wild, contradictory, and misleading rumors than were the circumstances of this investigation. The air was filled with all manner of tragic and absurd reports of what was doing and being done and going to be done elsewhere pertaining to the trial, but the crowd hung to the investigation with a tightening grip which no exciting tale of possible discomfiture could in the least degree relax, and on the morning of 21st of December the case opened with as large an attendance, and as firm a purpose as existed when it began. During arguments upon the admissibility of testimony many of the facts had been discussed, and the final arguments of the case were threshing over old straw. In these preliminary arguments Messrs. Davis and Smith had largely engaged, being gentlemen of ingenious talents and great plausibility of speech, and Messrs. Ritchie and Thurmond had somewhat reserved their efforts for the final arguments. If the rumors contemporaneous with the introduction of proof augmented the excitement to fever heat, the arguments of counsel added fuel to the flame. I cannot think that the testimony introduced to that assemblage left a particle of doubt in the mind of any spectator of the following five facts:

1st. That Ives killed Tbolt as charged.

2nd. That he had committed a half dozen other murders in the vicinity of equal cruelty.

3rd. That he was the leading actor in robbing the stage passengers between Rattlesnake Ranch and Bannack in October, when Dan McFadden, Leroy Southmayd, and others were passengers.

4th. That he had pursued the vocation of a highway robber for number of months along the roads leading to Salt Lake City.

5th. That he belonged to the Criminal classes, and that his

appetite for blood had grown till it became a consuming passion.

Ives' demeanor during the trial was quiet, and without apparent anxiety; he did not prejudice his case by any unmannerly demonstration, contrasting in this respect somewhat with his counsel, who at times seriously tried the patience of their auditors. The opening argument was by Mr. Bagg, and was a strong appeal to the citizens who had isolated themselves, and endured the hardships of mining and mining life to better their condition, now that they had certainly found one of the free-booters who infested the highways to make of him an example to all persons in like manner offending.

When the arguments opened I sent a note to Mr. John A. Creighton, a popular merchant at Virginia City, a king among the pioneers, telling him that the crisis had finally arrived, and asking him to bring with him all the good men he could find, and remain till the end.

The people of the West are very susceptible to the influence of speech, possibly not discriminating very closely as to its proprieties, and statements that an able speaker will occupy a given rostrum will attract more hearers in the West than elsewhere, and in that early day without newspapers or magazines or frequent occasions for oratory, such a symposium as was there promised attracted nearly every person in the Gulch to Nevada. The counsel for Ives were unquestionably discouraged with the strength of the case for the prosecution, at the poverty of their own resources for the defence and some humiliating exposures of the invalidity of the defence which they set up, and some of them indulged in libations much beyond what prudence would have dictated, though none but Mr. Ritchie seemed to have impaired their keenness of intellect by such indulgence. The hindrances during the progress of the trial seriously tried the patience of the miners, who were eager to return to the claims which they were opening to take advantage of the first rush of waters, and they interrupted counsel for the defence frequently by cat-calls and other signs of disapproval, feeling that their good nature and generosity were being imposed on, as indeed, in instances, was unquestionably true. I found frequent occasions to importune the crowd, whatever they felt was the provocation, to give them the amplest opportunity to say everything which they desired; an appeal which was, in every instance, I believe, successful. Occasionally there would burst from the throat of some witty spectator a remark which would set the crowd laughing, and sometimes a labored argument of a lawyer would be exploded by a common sense observation from some hard headed miner in the audience, who would wipe the labored structure of counsel off the boards in five words.

There was no bad temper in the crowd, except as to some of Ives' friends, but rather a stern purpose to see that complete justice was done, whatever and whoever stood in the way, and the passion grew as the speeches continued, and the hours waned.

Mr. Ritchie followed with an argument for his client, as good probably as could be made, but which did not, in my estimation, call for any special remark. He appealed to the softer side of human nature and clearly demonstrated that Tbolt could not be brought back to life, that everybody knew Ives was a clever fellow, generous and a little wild, and no one could tell what were the exact circumstances under which Tbolt was killed. Ives himself did not testify. Mr. Thurmond followed Mr. Ritchie, who, having become physically exhausted, repaired to some neighboring place of entertainment where liquid delights, as they are misnamed, were dispensed, and having somewhat over-estimated his capacity in that regard, during the balance of the arguments sat around muttering his discontent at the "outrages" which he saw in progress before him.

Thurmond was in many ways a masterful character; if a little coarse, he was strong in intellect. He had considerable pride to bring himself into the good opinion of those who met him, and his views generally agreed with, if they did not take their shape from the prevailing influences about him. His plea for Ives was able but it fell upon dull ears. A hundred or two men who would have been glad to see Ives acquitted more as a proof of their good-nature than otherwise, and the few who had been his companions in crime, at this stage of the proceedings constituted the outer portion of the crowd, whereas two days before they had been in its forefront.

The sun went down about the closing of the arguments, the night air became more chilly, and those habituated to drink made more frequent visits to the saloons, of which there were a great number in the streets and alleys of the little hamlet. The fire was blazing brightly, and by the directions of the judge, the twenty-four jurymen retired to a neighboring store to consider what their report should be. The audience remained standing, as of course they had been during the three days of the trial, but they did not disperse.

Illustrative of the methods by which counsel for the defence sought to obtain sympathy for their client, and prejudice the prosecution, both Mr. Thurmond and Mr. Ritchie had referred to me as "the gentleman from Oberlin." In some cases that might have been of assistance, but in this particular case it did not do them any good. No one at the present time can fully appreciate the stigma, contumely, and obloquy in such an audience ordinarily attaching to the epithet "Oberlin." Of course, it was not a geographical location, but an intellectual, political, ethnological expression, designed to be a "crusher" when less Herculean methods had failed. It had occurred, much to my regret, that although living within forty miles of that historic town, and having some acquaintance with its professors and students, I had never been able to attend a Commencement of President Finney's famous college. Indeed, except to be whirled through Oberlin on a swiftly moving train, I had never been there, but I was disinclined to enter a plea of "not guilty" and amid the cheers of the assembled multitude, four-fifths of whom hated the name, Oberlin got a certificate of character, which, if it did not do her any good, extracted the virus from the railing accusations which had been made against the counsel for the prosecution.

It was apparent from the opening of the trial that law and order, or order without law, had locked horns with crime, and that it was to be a fight to a finish. All through the trial I had been considering what course should be pursued when it was made manifest that Ives was guilty, and he should be so declared, and I had resolved inexorably that instant, if I could influence events, he should be consigned to swift destruction. The blood of too many desperate characters was up, and it seemed due to everybody connected with the prosecution that a vengeance so swift and so stern should follow his conviction as to cause it to be known that henceforth peaceable people would be in possession of their own. I felt instinctively that the trial would culminate in a situation of much delicacy.

The twenty-four jurymen returned to their benches with a report in writing that Ives was guilty of the murder of Tbolt as charged, but I do not remember whether they took cognizance of his other offences or no, and this report was signed by twenty-three jurors only; Henry Spivay declined to sign it not from any dissent, but for prudential reasons. The instant that report was read from the wagon, I made a motion, reciting that whereas George Ives for the murder of Nicholas Tbolt had been given a fair and impartial trial, with the privilege of being heard by council and witnesses, and had been reported to be guilty, that we approve of the verdict of the jury, and declare it to be the verdict of the miner's meeting, there assembled, and Judge Byam, without a moment's delay put my motion, and it was carried with a very loud shout, more than four-fifths of the citizens voting for the same. The significance of this movement did not seem to be appreciated by the defendant's counsel, and I instantly supplemented it with another motion, that George Ives, for the murder of which he was convicted, be now forthwith hung by the neck until he was dead. This motion being seconded, with equal promptness, Judge Byam put the motion and it was carried. It seems to me there was a feeble protest from Mr. Ritchie as to this last motion, to which it was replied that by the judgment of the meeting Ives had committed the murder, and punishment by hanging was the penalty. Whatever the facts were, there was no doubt as to the result, and Ives' friends, somewhat dazed by the swiftness with which these motions came, and the overwhelming support they received, turned their attention to an endeavor to have Long John hung at the same time.

Mr. Hereford and Mr. Davis were called to the wagon, and directed to carry the command of the meeting into immediate execution. Increasing the guard over Ives, who sat in a chair by the fire in front of the wagon, they went to find a suitable place to be used as a gallows. A cordon of pickets were stationed around the prisoner and the jury, all armed to the teeth, and the final event was awaited with profound expectancy the excitement momentarily increasing.

Ives finally arose from his seat, and came up into the wagon where I was standing. The excitement through the crowd was intense. A battle could scarcely have added anything to it. Ives came to me, and took me by the hand. If there was any tremor in his voice, or tremulousness in his person, I did not detect it, and the great crowd, always muttering something, was hushed into profound silence. For three days I had been expecting that this moment of exigency would arrive, and my mind was immovably made up as to what should be its outcome. Ives began by saying, "Colonel, I am a gentleman, and I believe you are, and I want to ask a favor which you alone can grant. If our places were changed, I know I would grant it to you, and I believe you will to me. I have been pretty wild away from home, but I have a mother and sisters in the States, and I want you to get this execution put off till tomorrow morning. I will give you my word and honor as a gentleman that I will not undertake to escape, nor permit my friends to try to change this matter."

I need not say that the appeal was one of great strength, but a simple event occurred, somewhat characteristic of the whole trial. One of the most noticeable, active and valuable men during its progress was a diminutive, short, young man acting as guard, vigilant, supple, observant, now here and now there wherever anything was to be done to secure the orderly conduct of the affair. He carried as did the majority of the crowd, a shotgun, the muzzle of which stood up a few inches above his head. He had gone from the crowd across the street, and climbed upon the dirt roof of a low log cabin where, from upon a ridgepole on the dirt, he was surveying from the rear the crowd surrounding the prisoner. Ives' request, spoken in an ordinary tone of voice, reached his ear, when he forthwith holloaed across the street, "Sanders, ask him how long a time he gave the Dutchman!," at which remark there was a ripple of laughter through the crowd, and while I had no thought to grant Ives' request and was reflecting in what manner of speech I should refuse it, and yet satisfy the sense of propriety of the miners, I have to confess that X. Beidler's remark lifted a considerable load from my mind. I replied to Ives, "You should have been thinking of this matter before. Get down there, maybe you can write a short letter to your folks before the sheriffs return for you. As to your property, I will make a motion which I think ought to satisfy you." He let go of my hand without response, jumped out of the wagon, sat down by the fire where some of his counsel were, and was furnished with a sheet of paper and a pencil, and proceeded to commence a letter to his mother.

I then moved that the Court take possession of Ives' property and dispose of it, pay the board of the guard and the prisoner during the days of the trial, and remit whatever remained to Ives' mother, which motion was assailed by Mr. Ritchie in very denunciatory terms, he saying that it was an outrage to murder a man, and make him pay the board of those who had participated in it. This was met by some remarks from some of the crowd, largely by way of interruption, and as the trial was over, I responded to Mr. Ritchie's denunciation by saying that it was not unusual to tax the cost of a case to the defendant against whom judgment of death was entered, and that if a lawyer was not aware of that fact I thought he should go to a law school instead of a law office. The motion was carried, but my remark had stirred to a profounder depth than I had anticipated the anger of Lawyer Ritchie.

I had worn during the trial a heavy overcoat with deep side pockets, in each of which I had carried a new Colt's police pistol for a number of months. As the excitement culminated about the time the jury retired, at the closing of the arguments, it occurred to me that possibly they had been loaded so long that they might not readily respond if I wanted to use them, and I thought it best to ascertain their condition. I threw my coat aside, and with my hand on my revolver, I pulled the trigger, and it went off clear as a bell. The effect was exciting, for shooting scraps were matters of momentary expectancy, and a number of persons around me were startled; however, the ball entering the ground, did no further damage than leaving a hole in the lining of my coat. Its effect upon me was a strengthening of confidence. The opposing counsel during the trial had in instances engaged in bluffs and rebuffs, and as the culmination drew near in personal denunciation, and there were bad men on the confines of the crowd, capable of any crime which passion or recklessness could suggest. Every man participating in that prosecution took his life in his hand, and those more prominently identified with it were the objects of much contumely and resentment from the friends of the highway robbers. Mr. Ritchie came to the side of the wagon and pulling my overcoat and with some profane expletives said that he wanted to see me, that we would settle this matter then and there. I alighted from the wagon, and he passed between two houses toward the rear, I following him, with an affair on my hands not pleasant nor wholly unexpected, but before we reached the rear of the houses, we were both seized by the sheriffs, or their assistants, and returned to the scene of the trial, where the excitement was unabated. Friends of Ives in considerable numbers were applying for permission to go inside the cordon of guards "to bid George Ives good-bye," and quite a number, some of them weeping bitterly, were granted the privilege.

Ives' effort to write a letter to his mother was interrupted by the excitement, and he did not finish it. In perhaps a half dozen lines of the fragment, he had written that he was surrounded by a mob who were going to hang him, and that he was seizing the few moments which remained of his life to write to her. If this was not the entire substance of what he wrote, it was practically the whole of it.

The sheriffs who had been gone for three-quarters of an hour, returned to report that they had been unable to find a convenient place to execute the orders of the miner's meeting, whereupon someone said most any place would answer, and suggested that an unfinished log building adjoining the one in front of which the trial was held would answer as well as any other place, and mounting to the top of the logs, which were not covered by any roof, he threw down one end of the top log, and with assistance it was placed at an angle of about 45 degrees, so that the upper end of it protruded into the street. A rope was procured from an adjacent store, and tied around the end of the log; the sheriffs procured a dry goods box, and Ives was placed upon it under the dangling rope.

It has been generally stated that Ives pulled off his boots, saying he had sworn that he would not die with his boots on. I do not remember this and only think it probable because it was told shortly thereafter, and I cannot say that I ever contradicted it, which I should think I would have done had it not been true. However, I have not written the details of this prosecution, nor have I attempted to speak of it in detail, now for the first time putting down with pen the events as I remember them, without consultation with any other authorities whatever. In fact the written authorities of Langford and Dimsdale are hearsay, neither one of these gentlemen having been present, but their information was gathered from actors in this stirring tragedy, and I consider them reliable. At least, where they differ from my own recollection, I find nothing inducing me to believe that there was any willful perversion of the facts.

As the denouement drew near the excitement increased, and

the anger of Ives' friends mounted higher and higher, manifesting itself in much profane denunciation of the proceedings. A guard of probably one hundred men surrounded the box on which Ives stood, facing outward, and beyond them was a crowd of miners and citizens, undiminished in numbers. The sheriff placed the rope around Ives' neck, and he was asked by the judge if he wished to say anything. When this had been accomplished his friends apparently abandoned all hope of saving him, and made a rush toward the warehouse in which John Frank and Hillerman were confined, swearing that Long John should be hung at the same time, but that prison was surrounded by a guard as resolute and grim as was Ives himself, and their effort ended in signal failure and profuse profanity. Ives said only a few words, I remember he said that he was not guilty of this crime, and when he had apparently finished, the dry goods box was tumbled from under him, and his friends broke forth into vile execrations toward those responsible for his taking off. The guard brought their guns down to the level, and there was a falling back of the crowd, but no dispersion of it, as it stood there for at least a half hour. The deed was done. Before there had been formal and perfunctory trials, amounting almost to challenges of the right of crime to rule in this region, but here there had been a strenuous controversy, a fair locking of horns between crime and order. It was yet to be determined, however, which should be master, for the disciples of disorder, discomfited, were by no means content to surrender to the reign of law. If not numerous, they were alert, active, defiant, and resourceful, and they did not intend to surrender at their first defeat. Many of them, intoxicated, breathed out threatenings and slaughter against prominent actors in the tragedy just closed, and they excited a wide apprehension that personal harm would come to me, and a guard of probably one hundred persons accompanied me to Virginia City, and in fact I was surrounded by a guard night and day for the week I remained in the Gulch.

The result of the trial among the miners, merchants, and other well disposed citizens was a subject of the profoundest congratulation. That evening I was in the store of Mr. John A. Creighton, with a number of gentlemen, conversing of the conditions surrounding the community, and listening to the turmoil of passion and hatred which seemed to have taken possession of the saloons, gambling houses, and dance houses along the street. Harvey Meade, a reputed desperado, who had escaped from the public justice of the Federal government at San Francisco, came into Mr. Creighton's wearing two revolvers in sight, and commenced an insolent conversation with me. It was said that he had been one of the conspirators to seize the revenue cutter *Chapman* in the interests of the Southern Confederacy, and to engage in piratical expeditions against Panama steamers and other commercial enterprises on the Pacific Ocean, which had been frustrated. The conspirators had escaped, and Meade turned up at Alder Gulch. I resented his insults somewhat, and for a moment there was evidence of dissent from his view. Dr. J. P. Maupin, who stood behind the counter, armed himself with a pick handle, but Mr. Creighton collared the braggadocio, and led him to the door, with warnings definite enough to be apprehended that he was expected to maintain peace.

I was the guest in Virginia City of Captain Nicholas Wall, who had erected a somewhat pretentious looking house at the rear of the store of John J. Roe and Co. which, with his nautical habit he had denominated "Texas," and which, for that time and place was an abode of no inconsiderable luxury. In the morning, upon awakening, I found four gentlemen outside the house guarding it on my account, of whom Mr.

X. Beidler: Vigilante

Michael Tovey and Conrad Weary were two, and guards remained with me and around my apartments until I left for Bannack.

At ten o'clock the next morning the meeting assembled again at Nevada for the disposition of the cases against George Hillerman and John Frank, but the strenuous controversy was over, the main criminal had been disposed of. Hillerman was an old weak, foolish man, doubtless without moral perception or cognizance of the crimes that were of daily occurrence and it was thought that, on the plane on which justice was administered at that time, it was not well to hang him, and after consultation with many of the leading citizens it was determined he should be banished and upon my motion it was made the duty of any person finding him in the settlements after New Year's to shoot him on sight. The lawyers reappeared with their passions somewhat allayed and their strenuousness perceptibly weakened, Messrs. Smith and Davis assuming the role of leading counsel for Hillerman. Hillerman desired to make a statement, and the privilege was granted him. He said nothing with reference to events in the country, but expressed a desire to be permitted to remain. He said he had no method of travel, and did not know how to go or where to go, to which a profane wit in the crowd responded by recommending to him a hot place beyond the confines of this world. The crowd, however, would not permit his presence, and he was ordered to go, with some arrangements made for his transportation, an opportunity of which he gladly availed himself, and his subsequent history is not known.

As to Long John, or John Frank, there was a universal belief that he had related truly such circumstances touching Tbolt's murder, and other murders and robberies in the country with frankness, and the animosity of the criminal

78

classes towards him consequent thereto, strengthened the resolve to permit him to live and remain in the country till he should choose to depart, and he was discharged on Fore-fathers' Day, 1863, and the miners dispersed to their claims, the merchants to their stores, and other citizens to their several places of business.

Four days had been expended by at least fifteen hundred men out of deference to the forms of American institutions, and when the prosecutions were finished, and the community knew no more than it did when they were begun, a number of people began to inquire whether each tragedy required so much attention, and how much time would be left to pursue the ordinary vocations if this deference was to be continued, and speculations as to forming a vigilance committee grew in coherence and strength. We had our confidence strengthened by the splendid fidelity of the miners of Alder Gulch, and by their unshaken resolve that that which they achieved they would preserve, despite the robbers who had so long infested the country, and on the evening of the next day, I think it was, the nucleus of a Vigilance committee was formed, there-after to grow to large proportions and to determine that in the heady struggle between order and crime, order should win the final mastery. But that is another story.

[V]

Vigilante Justice

IMMEDIATELY *after the hanging of Ives, five men met in Virginia City and four in Bannack and organized the Vigilantes. They met in the back room of a store kept by John Kinna and J. A. Nye. Paris S. Pfouts was made president; Wilbur F. Sanders, official prosecutor; and Captain James Williams, executive officer. Other members were William Clark and J. X. Beidler. Lights were extinguished and in total darkness the little group stood in a circle with hands uplifted while Sanders administered the oath:*

"We, the undersigned, uniting ourselves together for the laudable purpose of arresting thieves and murderers and recovering stolen property, do pledge ourselves on our sacred honor, each to all others, and solemnly swear that we will reveal no secrets, violate no laws of right, and never desert each other, or our standard of justice, so help us God."

[*Beidler's Journal resumes:*]

After the hanging of Ives, I was employed by Kiscadden, December 22nd, '63, to find their train which had been in distress. I started and went to Dailey's for dinner (where we got our daily bread) and camped with Mr. George Breckenridge that night. Next night camped out on White Tail— cold night—single blanket. Next day made Sage Creek—no house—Christmas Eve. As cold a night as I ever camped out in my life—danced around a green willow fire all night to the music of the coyotes and often thought during the night of

Montana State Historical Society

Vigilante headquarters, Virginia City, Montana

hundreds of other happy couples who were then dancing to other kinds of music. Next morning early, without eating, I started out to find Junction Ranche—found it at 11 A.M.

Next morning I went to the Hole in the Rock and met the train—train very poor and dying—had to have fresh cattle. Stayed over night and started back next day. Camped in Quaking Asp near Toll Gate and got a bottle of gin, then arrived at Toll Gate and towards evening saw a white man coming towards camp, which turned out to be Dutch John [Wagner] and an Indian.

When I was at Beaver Head I heard that Forbes' train had been attacked by two robbers and that they were repulsed. One was shot in the shoulder and the other in the back. I was given the description of the men. I was looking for them. One was described as having a fine beaded pair of leggings, which I said if I found would be mine. Dutch John's both hands were badly frozen and I asked: "How is it that a big husky like you gets froze and this Injun is O. K.? Why don't you flop your wings and keep warm?"

I got a gold pan and filled it with spring water and made him hold his hands in it but the pain was too severe. He drank my bottle of gin. While I was taking the frost out of his fingers and he was drinking my gin, he asked me where I was from and how times were in Salt Lake. He said he was going to Ricker's Ferry. I told him I had not been to Salt Lake, but was from Virginia City. When he heard I was from there, he got frightened and acted very uneasy and wanted to know if George Ives was hung yet. I told him I helped hang him and he got very reticent.

I told him of Forbes' train having been robbed. He asked me if they had got the robbers. I told him, "No not yet," and that I understood one of them had a fine pair of leggings on, and when I found them I was going to appropriate them.

"Why," he said, "would you have taken them?"

I said: "Yes, if I found the man dead."

He took another smile out of the gin bottle and looked at me wilder than a wolf. During all this time I had almost got the frost out of his hands and him pretty well braced up.

We retired for the night on the floor and in the morning his hands were all blistered and I got some balsam and fixed them up the best I could. I then started alone to Virginia City and they started for Ricker's Ferry on Snake River.

When I got to the top of Pleasant Valley Divide, I saw a party of ten or fifteen horsemen and packs on their way to Salt Lake with 200 pounds of gold dust as freight. Being acquainted with them, they asked me if I had seen Dutch John. Told them I had just left him, and had tied up his frozen hands. They asked me to go back and capture him and take him to Bannack, as he was wanted for holding up Forbes' train and was one of the wounded robbers. I told them I had no time and had to attend to the business of the distressed train first. I camped that night at the junction on my way home.

From Junction I went to Horse Prairie and on my way I met George Hilderman, who was banished when George Ives was hung. He knew me and I warned him to turn out of the trail. He wanted to know if it was safe for him to keep going. I assured him it was, and to keep a-going.

Next day I went into Bannack and at night I went down town and at Durant's Saloon played a game of billiards and old man Gilman came in and asked where I stopped. He told me to go right off and stay there. I wanted to know why and he told me that Buck Stinson and the gang were in town and had it in for me and would kill me. I hesitated, but finally went. Told proprietor of hotel what was up, but on my way there I met Buck Stinson and Ned Ray, and they asked me where I was going. I told them. I stayed in the hotel all night.

In the morning I had early breakfast and started in a bad snow storm towards Rattlesnake Creek. When I got there, who should I meet but Buck Stinson and the gang. I was cold and stiff and had a bottle of brandy in my pocket. Went to the room and got warmed up and saw Andy Lewis, a friend of mine, the only man I could count on as a friend.

The gang asked me up to the bar and I said: "Gentlemen, I have a bottle of brandy of my own and I prefer drinking that."

After supper we got to talking about Vigilantes and they wanted to know how many of them there were. I said no less than a thousand if there were any, and they wanted to know what they wanted so many for. I told them: "It would take a thousand to let decent people live here."

That night Andy and I made our bed down together. Buck and his party barricaded the door with the table. I asked them what that was for and they said: "We expect the Vigilantes tonight and we will hold you for hostage."

Buck got up several times in the night and I followed suit every time.

In the morning Buck asked me where I was going. Told him I thought I would stay over a day. They saddled up and lit out down Rattlesnake Creek, and as soon as they were out of sight, we saddled up and lit out for Virginia.

When out about ten miles we met a party of eight men coming toward us. They hollered for us to throw up our hands which we didn't do as we recognized our friend, Tom Baume's voice, and told him he might as well kill a man as scare him to death.

That night we camped at Dempsey's ranche. I gave them the information about Buck Stinson being at Rattlesnake where the eight men went right away. At Dave Pickett Lodge they got Erastus Yager, known as "Red," bringing him back to Dempsey's. At Dempsey's we picked up George Brown, secretary to the road agents.

"Red" confessed. He said to us: "You have treated me like a gentleman and I know I am going to die. I am going to be hanged."

He told us that Henry Plummer was chief of the road agents and Bill Bunton was next to him. Others of the gang were Sam Bunton who was sent away for being a drunkard, Cyrus Skinner, Stephen Marshland, Dutch John Wagner, Aleck Carter, Whiskey Bill Graves, Johnny Cooper, Ned Ray, Bab Zachery, Mexican Frank, Frank Parish, Boone Helm,[1] and Club-foot George, Haze Lyons, Bill Hunter, George Lowry, Billy Page, "Doc" Howard, Jem Romaine, Billy Terwillinger, and Ged Moore.

We hung both of these men at Lorraine's on a cottonwood tree.

Brown begged for mercy and died praying. Yager shook hands with us and his last words were: "Good-bye. God bless you. You are on a good undertaking."

Then we went on to Bannack to get Plummer, Stinson, and Ray.

[*On the 23rd of December, the day after X. Beidler went to the relief of Kiscadden's train, twenty-four men started out on a secret expedition. The wives of married members had no idea of their destination or purpose. They were armed, carried rations, blankets, and rope. No one knew when they departed. The weather was bitterly cold. There had been a deep fall of snow. They suffered, for no fires could be kindled. A campfire might have betrayed their presence and defeated their purpose.*

[1] Beidler sometimes spells this name "Boon."

X. Beidler: Vigilante

They met "Red" (so called from his fiery hair and whisk-ers) Yager, on Deer Lodge Creek. He told them that Aleck Carter, an accomplice of George Ives in the Tbolt murder, "Whiskey Bill," and other members of the gang, were drunk at Dempsey's Cottonwood Ranch.

While the Vigilantes rode to Dempsey's, the road agents were making a swift get away over the Divide. Yager had warned them to "get up and dust and look out for black ducks." They lost no time until they put seventeen miles of difficult mountain trails between them and their pursuers. When the Vigilantes reached Cottonwood Ranch, the birds had flown. Bold in their defiance, they kindled a campfire to signal their escape.

The Vigilantes, disheartened at apparent defeat, decided to return by Beaver Head Rock. It was still bitter cold. Their horses stampeded. Rations were short. Then they met X. Beidler and Andy Lewis. They informed X that they were hunting for Carter, Stinson, Ray, and any other road agents at large and unhung.

Another atrocious murder had been committed. The vic-tim was Lloyd Magruder, a beloved man who was candidate for Congress. During the summer of 1863, he brought a pack train of merchandise to Virginia City and opened a store. The result was a profit of $14,000. He determined to return to Lewiston, via Elk City. C. Allen, Horace and Robert Chalmer, and a Mr. Phillips were to accompany him. The news of Mag-ruder's journey with $14,000 in gold dust to Lewiston became current news. Plummer and his gang met in Alder Gulch and planned the robbery of the pack train and the murder of Magruder and his friends. They planned to have Jem Ro-maine, "Doc" Howard, Billy Page, and one Bob or Bill Lowry join the party, murder the five members, then steal the gold dust.

Vigilante Justice

Magruder was an ingenuous man and he trusted every-body. When the road agents expressed a desire to join him, he offered them "free passage" and through tickets on mule-back! The journey was uneventful until they camped near the Bitter Root Mountains beyond Clearwater River. The horses were turned loose to graze. Magruder and Bill Lowry went out to watch them. They built a fire, and as Magruder bent over to light his pipe, Lowry split his skull with an ax. The plot had been well thought out. At ten o'clock, the hour agreed upon by the road agents, the four other victims were murdered in their sleep in the main camp. Only one cried out. The gold dust was taken by the robbers, the bodies of the murdered men rolled up in an old canvas and dumped over a precipice, the camp equipment burned, and all but the finest eight horses driven off into a cañon and shot. The murderers wore moccasins, thinking that if intruders discovered traces of crime before obliterating snow flew, it would be attributed to Indians.

Magruder's mule, saddle leggings, and other possessions were recognized at Elk City. Later, at Lewiston, Magruder's objective on the fatal trip, Hill Beechy, deputy marshal and owner of the Luna House, observed the cantinos *of newly ar-rived travelers overflowing with gold dust, and suspected that the road agents had made another kill. Just as they boarded a stage coach for San Francisco, a man named Goodrich recognized Page. Beechy followed him and his companions to California. There he arrested them for the murder of Mag-ruder and his companions and the robbery of the pack train. Page turned state's evidence, told the details of the plot and the crime, and incriminated Henry Plummer, chief and Master Mind of the road agents and sheriff of two districts! After a fair trial all of the murderers, except Page, were hanged.*

87

X. Beidler: Vigilante

The capture of Plummer was the next move of the Vigilantes.]

[*Frank Gallagher was next captured. This event is described by an eye-witness, Chauncey Barbour, in the* Dillon Tribune, *September 16, 1887, and is quoted by X. Beidler:*]

One cold winter morning I was in Virginia City, Montana, had breakfasted and was about to start up the Gulch to my home about eight miles above, when suddenly a battalion of armed men appeared at the lower end of the main street. I saw them march in perfect order up the street a hundred yards or so, halt and receive some orders, and disperse in squads. I started home, but was stopped outside the city by a *posse* of a dozen men and informed that I could not pass. Their orders were that no one could go, but anyone might come in. I knew some of them—one in fact was my partner. But they were inexorable. They pointed out, and I saw a cordon of just such *posses* posted closely all around the city.

The military squads were scouring the city. I followed one squad, under old man Clark, into a large saloon called the California Exchange. It had been a sort of headquarters of the gang. He demanded of the barkeeper if any of the "men on his list" were around there. The barkeeper said: "No."

"Very well, we propose to search these premises," said the old man.

Thereupon the barkeeper admitted that there was one of them in the back room, on a bed there, with a double-barreled shotgun loaded with buckshot on each side of him, and a whole battery of revolvers belted around him. He volunteered also the statement that he had passed through the saloon just after the Committee appeared and said they were after him and it meant death, but he would send half a dozen of them to hell before they got him.

Upon this, some of the young men with Clark started to the rear; but the old man ordered them to come back and guard the place, while he fetched out the prisoner. He pooh-poohed the idea of danger. I disagreed with him and cocked my ears for the expected cannonade, as I saw the old man disappear in the rear with a revolver in his hand.

I was wrong, for soon he reappeared, grasping by the collar a livid wretch whose knees were knocking together. I looked, and lo! it was my quondam acquaintance, Jack Gallagher. He saw me, and a gleam of hope shot across his face as he implored me for God's sake to do something for him. I told him I could do as much against a whirlwind with a fence rail, and turned away.

I asked old man Clark afterward about the arrest and told him I actually thought the man would at least sell his life dearly. I had seen and heard of some of them standing up and banging away bravely enough.

"No, sir," said he, "they are all cowards at heart. Their courage is whiskey courage, and they are only brave when they have far the best of it."

I think the simple philosophy of the old gentleman the correct one. Honor and justice have such an ascendancy over crime that when they confront it squarely it invariably wilts.

The perquisitions of the Committee in Virginia City that day realized five of the men on their list—one man named Bill Hunter escaping by hiding in an empty barrel that was standing among some filled ones in a warehouse cellar. He crawled out in the dead of night, and his tracks in the snow where he had betaken himself to the mountains were found next day. The poor wretch was afterward found in a deserted cabin a hundred miles away, where he died a horrible death.

[*E. J. Porter in the* Helena Independent, *March 24, 1886, describes the events that followed:*]

X. Beidler, with a detachment of the Vigilantes of Virginia City, came over to Bannack immediately after the hanging of Haze Lyons, Jack Gallagher, Frank Parish, Boone Helm, and Club-foot George, the five men mentioned. They arrived late one Saturday night; I think it was the 12th of January, 1864. There was about two feet of snow on the ground, the weather was very cold, and their sudden appearance in such weather and at so late an hour, aroused the suspicions of many of the citizens.

The next morning, which was Sunday, they proceeded to organize, very quietly, a vigilance committee, and guards were placed around the town the same day, to prevent the escape of the ringleaders and desperadoes of the gang who had been condemned by the law abiding portion of the citizens.

On Sunday evening, shortly after dark, I was approached by Mr. Wiles, a citizen of Bannack, stating that he desired me to join the vigilantes. I at first declined to join until I had some further explanation of the matter, and he left me, but returned in half an hour and handed me a double-barrel shotgun, requesting me to join them in arresting Plummer, Stinson, and Ray. As soon as I knew it was for that purpose, I at once assented, and went along, and we met the other members of the committee at an appointed place. We numbered in all seventeen men, all armed with double-barrel shotguns well loaded.

I had arrived in Bannack on the 15th of August, 1862. About thirty-five men were in the camp at that time, and about thirty men were in our party. Most of us took up claims and went to mining. Henry Plummer and Buck Stinson came into the camp late in the fall. Shortly after Plummer's arrival he shot and killed a former traveling companion of his, from Walla Walla, named Jack Cleveland, in a saloon in Bannack. The form of a trial was gone through, but which was a mere mockery of justice, and Plummer was acquitted of this cold blooded murder, but very narrowly escaped lynching by the citizens.

After this tragedy everything seemed to move along quietly for some time, and the following winter several parties came in from Walla Walla and various other places. The mines had been paying well and there was plenty of money in the camp.

During the summer of 1863 a great many robberies were committed in and around Bannack and of the stage and express lines, and a number of murders were committed. Among the number was George Carhart, who was shot while asleep in his bed, but it was not known who killed him.

The stampede to Alder Gulch took place in the spring of 1863. Buck Stinson also went to Virginia City and was engaged in several killing scrapes, and was banished from there and came back to Bannack the same year.

In the fall of 1863, Ned Ray arrived from Salt Lake City, where he broke jail.

During the spring of 1863 an election was held in Bannack, at which Henry Plummer was elected sheriff by the worst element of the community. The first notable act of his was to arrest a man [named Horan] for shooting another. He had a gallows erected and hung him the same day.

During the summer of 1863, Plummer became the leader of a numerous gang of outlaws and desperadoes, and being also Sheriff he had plenty of opportunities to play into their hands, and work to the advantage of this dangerous element of the community. And as before stated many robberies were committed by "holding up" the coaches on the road from Bannack, through Virginia City to Salt Lake, so that in the fall it became almost impossible for anyone to leave Bannack without being waylaid and robbed. Buck Stinson was known to be one of this band of thieves and murderers.

Early in the fall, "Old Snag," the chief of the Bannack tribe of Indians, with a party of his tribe, being on his way back from the Yellowstone, where he had been on the war path, was shot and killed by Stinson, and his scalp was taken by Skinner, a saloon-keeper (who was afterwards hung in Deer Lodge), and hung up in his saloon as one of his trophies. Skinner was the great slugger and knock-down champion of the gang, which had now become so powerful and numerous that no one dared to express himself in opposition for fear of being set upon, and beaten, and abused, and perhaps killed. This condition of things continued through the fall and into mid-winter.

Sometime during 1863 a vigilance committee was organized at Virginia City in Alder Gulch. A great many bad men were hung there.

We were informed that Stinson had started to go to church with his wife. We went in the direction of Bill Toulson's house and found him there and arrested him. We next went for Plummer, and arrested him and took him along also to a hall where we found Ned Ray, and arrested him. None of them made any resistance, and we bound their hands and arms and took up our line of march with the prisoners for the same gallows which Plummer had erected to hang Horan.

This was about eight o'clock in the evening. It was quite dark, but as we approached the gallows we could see three ropes dangling from the crossbeam. We halted a few feet from the gallows and told the prisoners if they had anything to say to do so at once as their time was short. They all proclaimed their innocence, saying that they had not done anything to be hung for. Plummer said he wanted a fair trial, but he was told that he had had his trial, and the only trial he would now have would be at the end of a rope.

Ned Ray was the first victim, and when requested to walk under the rope he said: "Hold on, I want to pray." He also said he wanted to take his coat off, and made an attempt to do so, but could not. As he did not proceed to pray, the rope was placed around his neck and the order was given to pull up, which was done with such force that it came very near upsetting the gallows. The rope was slackened again and he remarked: "Hold on, d——n it, you are choking me!"

Nothing more was said, and the order was again given to pull up, which was accordingly done and the poor wretch expired after a few struggles.

Buck Stinson's turn came next. He said nothing that I can recollect, only to declare his innocence. The rope was drawn and he died almost without a struggle.

During this time Plummer became awfully alarmed, and was walking around inside the circle formed by the vigilantes, begging those among them whom he knew to help him and imploring them to let him off, promising that if they did so he would leave the country.

The turbulent, brutal man, who could shoot down and kill or hang others without remorse, when he had the advantage, now that the scales were turned and he was placed in the same condition, cowered and quailed in the presence of death and cried like a child. He made very strong appeals to Crissman and McDonald for help, but they replied: "No, Henry, we can't do anything for you."

The rope was placed around his neck, and the wretched Plummer was slowly raised and strangled to death.

93

X. Beidler: Vigilante

The vigilantes remained about half an hour longer, when, after the physician pronounced the victims dead, they retired for the night, and left the bodies hanging until morning.

The next morning the same committee, with many other citizens, went to the cabin of a Mexican, Joe Pizanthia, "The Greaser," a violent and notorious character from Virginia City. Judge Copley and four other men entered his cabin to arrest him, but did not at once find him. Copley, with his gun, raised the curtain that hung around his bed, to look under it in search of the Mexican, who it appears had hidden underneath and had two revolvers in his hands. He instantly fired at Judge Copley, the ball taking effect in his abdomen, and proving fatal after ten hours of intense suffering. They all retired to the outside of the cabin. The Mexican came to the door and fired into the crowd, wounding Smith Ball in the knee. Governor Edgerton gave the citizens the privilege of using a mountain howitzer belonging to the government, with which to shell the cabin. The first shot passed entirely through the cabin, but the second one exploded inside, making a wreck of it and wounding the Mexican. The door was knocked down and had fallen on his prostrate body. Five men entered the cabin and placed a rope around his neck and dragged the body out and hung him to a clothes post.

The cabin was at once demolished—the logs all piled up, fire was set to the logs and the body of the Mexican was thrown into the fire and that was the end of "The Greaser," Joe Pizanthia. The next morning some ghoulish prostitutes panned out the ashes of the dead hoping to find gold.

A few days after this, Neil Howie,[2] who was afterwards United States Marshal of Montana Territory, arrested John Wagner, a notorious highway robber. He was brought to Bannack and hung.

[2] Beidler sometimes spells this name "Neill."

Vigilante Justice

[Beidler's Journal resumes:]

In the fall of 1863, a certain Henry Brent was tried before the Vigilantes. Circumstantial evidence seemed to show that he was one of the road agents, and he was ordered out of the Territory. Brent said he was innocent. He was a young man whose talk and behavior showed that he came from a good family. Crying, he left the judges, took his horse and lit out. It was in the evening as we finished our work, hung two and ordered Brent out of the Territory. The 20 Vigilantes then went to our different homes.

John Stuart, James Arneaux, J. J. Healy, and I had to ride 60 miles to get home. About ten o'clock at night, we heard a shot fired close to us and several other shots followed. We dropped from our horses and skirmished around to find out what was the matter. We saw a man on horseback hollering and recognized the man Brent who had been ordered out. Brent said that about 50 Indians were following and we had better turn back. Then we went up a little hill and Brent with us. The Indians came and the fight commenced. Brent was shot and he fell. Then the Indians retired. As soon as they were out of sight, we went to Brent and took care of him, laid him under a tree, washed him and gave him something to drink. Then Brent commenced to talk and said: "Save yourselves and let me die. I cannot walk or ride. During the night you can escape but if you wait until daylight you may all be killed."

Jim Arneaux, with his rifle in his hand, went up a cleft to look after the horses. The rest of us built a camp fire near Brent and lay down on the grass.

"Save yourselves comrades. I am too weak to escape," said Brent.

X. Beidler: Vigilante

John Stuart said: "We will stay with you now. Under the circumstances we cannot leave you."

Brent asked him again: "Let me die alone. My life is not worth saving. As a convict you have ordered me out of the Territory and among honorable people I am not fit to live."

"It is settled," said Stuart. "So long as we can stay with you we will defend you."

"Thanks Cap't. You think I am a road agent, but I swear by the grave of my dear Mother that I am innocent. Believe me before it is too late so that I can die easy," said Brent.

I said: "We believe you are innocent." The others agreed.

"Then I can die easy," said Brent. He drew his pistol and shot himself.

The four of us were now standing by the young man who killed himself to let us escape.

On the hill where Brent died is a cross with the following inscription: *"Here died a brave young man to save others their lives."*

[VI]

The Hanging of Slade

BEFORE Slade was hung at Virginia City, I met him at different times and places, and we were friends.

I met him at his ranch on the Madison River when he lived in a tent and his wife cooked a good dinner for us. We communed on many occasions as friends. Slade was an honest man and did not like a thief, but was a very dangerous man when drinking.

The day before he was hung, Kiscadden and I walked across the Washington Billiard Hall (drinks and billiards 50 cents, everybody busy). Kiscadden was a friend of Slade's and they got into a conversation and not being interested, I got up to go out when Slade shouted out: "God damn you, where are you going? Are you afraid?"

I told him I was not interested in the conversation and that I had the privilege to go where I wanted to and that I did not have to go.

When the people in the saloon heard Slade and I having these words everybody rushed out of the saloon, thinking our guns would go off and someone get hurt sure and were afraid of any stray balls catching them.

Slade saw the consternation of the people in the saloon but did not see me move and he said: "X come back," which I did and he then asked me to take a drink. I said I would sooner do that than fight.

We went to the bar—Johnny Tomlinson was bartender—and we all took whiskey straight,—Kiscadden, Slade, and

97

myself. After we got our glasses filled and were going to drink, Slade, still mad, said: "You do not have to drink unless you want to"—meaning that I could fight instead.

I said: "Mr. Slade that is another privilege and I will not drink."

By this time the people who had stampeded out at our first growl were getting in again when they saw us going to drink, but when they again heard our talk they again rushed out like a flock of sheep in a great hurry with a band of wolves behind them. During this stampede Slade had insulted the barkeeper, Tomlinson, and he raised a big Colt's navy revolver in front of Slade and declared himself to take a hand in the fight and Slade then weakened and said: "Let us quit."

I told him I was glad, knowing well that right behind me stood at least six of Slade's pals and fighters and anyone that hurt Slade was going to be killed instantly.

When Slade had quit and left, I turned to Kiscadden and asked him if he had brought me into the saloon to get into a fuss with Slade. He denied having done so, which I believed, and we left.

I went and told my friends and the Slade men that we had a fuss and that if it occurred again I should certainly take care of myself and that I was going to the Theater where Kate Harper was acting that evening ($2 ½ a ticket).

The Theater was crowded with men with their wives and daughters, who had come to see the acting. In the play, Kate Harper came out on the stage dressed as a Ballet girl to give a dance and as she commenced Slade ordered her in a loud and vulgar voice to take off the balance of her dress, which disgusted the audience and they commenced leaving. Men with their wives and daughters could not stay. The show ended right there and I avoided Slade that evening as well as I could and I did not see him after the Theater.

The Hanging of Slade

Next morning Slade was still running wild and run a milk wagon off the grade and spilled all the milk and then went and whipped Dan Harding and Charley Edwards, his own men, then came uptown and run it for all it was worth. Merchants closed their stores to avoid trouble and Slade held the Fort. I went to Jerry Sullivan, who is now in Butte, and asked him if he couldn't get Slade to go home. Jerry said he couldn't touch him. I went to Kiscadden and asked him if he could get Slade home. Just at this time Slade came into the store and said: "X, I guess the Vigilance Committee is played out."

I said: "It looks so but you will change your mind in three hours."

He looked at me very enquiringly with those eyes of his and asked how I knew. I told him he would see, and I again asked Kiscadden to try to coax him to go, and Slade said he would if Kiscadden would give him his Derringer, which he did and I then told Slade to get on his favorite horse, old "Copperbottom" and cross the hill, which he did. He rode a short distance, and got off "Copperbottom," at Pfouts' store and insulted him in a very disgusting manner.

While he was hard at work doing this dirty work, over two hundred honest, determined miners headed by Capt. Williams were just turning the corner and getting in sight, and came up to Pfouts' store. Capt. Williams stepped up and arrested Slade while he was holding up Pfouts, Fox, and Davis with a Derringer in each hand. Capt. Williams was backed by two hundred miners, each one of which could have shook out two or three dollars of pay dirt out of the rims of their hats, and who had rifles and revolvers in abundance. Slade looked around and said: "My God!"

He was informed he had one hour to live and if he had any business to attend to he had better do it. I was well aware of the approach of the Committee and was informed long before that the boys' rifles and revolvers were being cleaned and loaded fresh, which meant business. I had begged Slade to go home but I knew when he got off his horse, and I made the remark to Kiscadden, that it was his last ride. If Slade had gone off when he was told, the Committee would not have hung him at that time.

Slade was taken into the back room of the store to settle up his business and begged all the time most piteously for his life.

A party was sent to arrange a place for the execution. They went down the Gulch and found an empty beef scaffold, made the noose and fixed everything for the hanging, and when the hour given by the Committee to Slade had expired Slade expired with it.

The town was very excited, people running to and fro and not knowing the result of the Committee's business—if Slade was King, or if the Vigilantes had won. But very little talk was going on. Each man of the Committee kept place with determination and his mouth shut but the determination on their lips soon let the people know that Slade was hung.

While Slade was standing on the boxes, under the scaffold, with the rope around his neck, he asked for Col. W. F. Sanders, and the boys around were afraid to do much shouting and I said: "Boys, pass the word along for Sanders," which was done, but he could not be found and Slade then asked for Aleck Davis, who came up and talked with the doomed man.

Slade asked Davis to plead with the crowd for his life and Davis said: "Mr. Slade I can only repeat your words, I have no influence but would gladly do so if I had."

The two hundred miners were getting impatient and shouted: "Time's up!" These men were running mines on their own account and wanted to get back and clean up and attend to their business as they did not come on any child's play.

A noble German by the name of Brigham adjusted the rope around Slade's neck and afterwards left the Territory, being afraid of the Slade men. Dutch Charley selected the place for the execution.

Capt. Williams, when he heard how impatient the miners were getting, said "Men do your duty." And Slade died.

During the hanging of Slade I was stationed upon the bench and was looking down the Gulch, and a man whose initials are N. T. pulled his rifle and said he would kill any man who helped hang Slade, and knelt down keeping his rifle ready to shoot.

I told him that the smoke would not get away from him before he was riddled by twenty bullets and as I spoke I saw him covered with rifles of members of the Committee in a second. He didn't shoot, fortunately for him.

Mrs. Slade had been sent for and was expected every minute and she was known to be a very desperate woman and the Committee had wisely ordered some parties to intercept her if she came before the hanging. Jim Kiscadden came to me and said: "X, can't I get men enough to cut Slade down before Mrs. Slade gets here?"

I got some friends of mine and I cut him down and we packed him to the Virginia City Hotel and took the ropes off his legs, arms and feet, and just as I was through, someone said: "Mrs. Slade is coming!"

I threw a blanket over the things to hide them from her and she rushed into the room and threw herself on the body of her dead husband. I went down stairs. The miners returned to their work and the town quieted down and peace reigned. Slade was neatly dressed and prepared for burial and taken across the hill and buried and was afterwards taken to Salt

Lake. Mr. Kiscadden afterwards married Mrs. Slade. The Slade men dispersed as their leader was gone and they had seen a lesson.

[VII]

Stagecoach Robbery

IN THE APRIL following, I helped escort Kiscadden, Dr. Glick, and others who were going East with 400 pounds of gold dust. When we got into camp at White Tail Creek we ran across Sheriff Fox and wife—the man that Slade took a warrant from and tore it up. His wife was supposed to have stolen some money from a man by the name of Edgar and he and Sheriff Burt Cavan overtook them at this camp and went through the party. We traveled together until the Salt Lake Road ran to the right and Soda Butte Road to the left. They went to Salt Lake City, camped next night on Sage Creek, and found we had lost a ham off the wagon which Kiscadden raised such a fuss about, that I saddled up and went back after it and found a wolf had it and was just taking his supper off it. I took it from him and went back to camp.

When we got back to Snake River, we ran across George Hilderman. He tried to approach our camp disguised as a squaw. He had a load of brush on his back. We fired him and told him if he came within shot of camp again we would kill him.

We forded Snake River next day and went on down to Soda Springs and there Kiscadden put the gold on pack animals and went on to Bridger. We came back to Virginia from there but lost our mules on the way.

At Virginia City about Christmas, 1863, Kinny and McCassland had a store and were doing a fine business, when some trouble occurred between them and they had a quarrel. Mc-Cassland shot Kinny. McCassland was arrested and I put him in gaol where he remained until the Spring term and was acquitted. He then settled his business, which took some time as he was worth lots of money and then he left Virginia City for Salt Lake in company with Mr. Parker, Dave Dinan, Mr. Carpenter, Mr. Brown, and some others. The party had $60,000 in gold dust with them in the coach. When they got to Snake River they became alarmed as things did not look exactly right—too much talking outside. They then thought they would hire a freight team to go through Portneuf Cañon, Idaho, with—kind of slip through—and leave the coach. Frank Williams, the driver of the coach, assured them there was no danger—took his word for it and continued on the stage.

On July 13, Parker was sitting outside with the driver, the rest inside the 6-horse big Concord Coach. When they had got into the cañon 6 or 8 miles to a place known as Hell's Half Acre there was a high water road and a summer road. The driver took the lower road (the first time that summer).

Parker saw the road agents in the willows and hollered: "Boys, here they are!"

The team dashed up to the road agents and stopped. Parker fired one shot at them and then fell dead. The road agents poured a volley into the coach shooting both feet off Charley, the messenger on the coach, and killed 3 of the passengers inside. The team by this time had got unmanageable from so much shooting going on and had started on the run and tore the tongue out of the wagon. Mr. Carpenter, who was in the bottom of the coach with 3 dead men on top of him, lay there. Brown, during this time, got out and skipped to the thick brush. The robbers went through the coach and got the money and took the watches from these men. After they had got all the valuables and walked away, one of the road agents said: "I don't believe that s—— of a b—— at the bottom of the coach is dead," and said he would go fix him—he might squeal.

They went back and saw him. Carpenter said: "Gentlemen, I am dying. Don't mutilate my face so my wife can recognize me when I am taken to Salt Lake."

This was about three o'clock P.M. and there was some freight teams close at hand and they knew that Brown was in the willows so they took the swag and lit out upon their horses which were tied close by. The dead were taken care of and buried.

When the news arrived at Virginia City it caused a terrible excitement—the coach came back literally filled with bullets. The Vigilance Committee were very anxious to capture the road agents and sent our several parties all over the country, but without success. Immediately after the robbery, the driver quit working and went to Salt Lake, turning up there with a heap of money—a man who had never saved a dollar of his wages. He would buy suits of clothes for any old stage driver he would meet in Town and squander money by the handfull. We had him spotted. He bought a diamond ring.

There was a prisoner in gaol whom we had banished for robbing Arbour's Saloon in Virginia City and the Shade Saloon. He was supposed to be an expert on diamonds and Frank Williams took this diamond for him to examine it. This man found out in some way that Williams was in the robbery in Portneuf Cañon—sent to one of Fargo's men and said that if they would help him out of gaol, he would tell them something. They agreed to help him out. He then gave Williams away. Williams got on to it and pulled out for Denver.

The Committee at Virginia City held a council and sent Dutch Charley to Salt Lake to follow Williams. He was captured near Denver by Dutch Charley, Maj. Reed, and others and was hung near that place.

His capture was made principally by the efforts of the Vigilance Committee of Virginia City. The balance of the robbers have not been found and Williams would not give up their names.

[VIII]

Cleaning Up

[AFTER THE HANGING *of Slade, the law-abiding citizens of the Territory of Montana enjoyed comparative peace until 1865. During that year a series of outrages occurred. As a result the Vigilantes again asserted their dreaded authority. A local newspaper printed this item:*]

The following admonition to the "dangerous classes," appeared posted about town, and unless we are mistaken in our conjectures, the committee mean just what they say. A reputation for honesty and peaceable demeanor, is not to be held lightly in these stirring times:

NOTICE

TO ALL WHOM IT MAY CONCERN:
Whereas divers foul crimes and outrages against the persons and property of the citizens of Montana have been lately committed and whereas, the power of the civil authorities, though exerted to its full extent, is frequently insufficient to prevent their commission, and to punish the perpetrators thereof; now, this is to warn and notify all whom it may concern that the Vigilance Committee, composed of the Citizens of the Territory, have determined to take these matters into their own hands, and to inflict summary punishment upon any and all malefactors in every case, where the civil authorities are unable to enforce the proper penalty of the law.

The practice of drawing deadly weapons, except as a last

resort, for the defense of life, being dangerous to society and in numerous instances leading to affrays and bloodshed, notice is hereby given, that the same is prohibited and offenders against this regulation will be summarily dealt with. In all cases the Committee will respect and sustain the action of the civil authorities.

This notice will not be repeated, but will remain in full force and effect from this date.

September 19, 1865

VIGILANCE COMMITTEE

[Beidler's Journal resumes:]

In 1865 a train of emigrants were on their way to Virginia City, Montana, and in the Indian country Wm. Hoffstettler killed Mr. Frazier, about some quarrel over a cabin. Frazier approached Hoffstettler with a hatchet in his hand in the evening, by the camp fire. Hoffstettler pulled his six-shooter and killed Frazier. The train continued on to Virginia City after burying Frazier, Hoffstettler and Frazier's son being with the train. In Virginia City Frazier's son met G. M. Pinney and made complaint against Hoffstettler in U. S. Court. In the meantime Hoffstettler got scared and lit out. I, with the warrant for his arrest, pursued him and, never having seen him, got a description of him from young Frazier. I captured him near the Benson Ferry on the Yellowstone. He was going back to the States—down the Yellowstone. I passed several men but they did not answer the description. Finally I came up with one that came pretty near it, and I said: "Hello, Mr. Hoffstettler, how do you do?"

He stuck out his hand and was going to shake, but I told him to hold up his little hands and he said he had nothing. I told him I had a ticket for him to go back with me to Virginia City. I had an extra horse along, and we started back.

Cleaning Up

His baggage, etc., he sent on to the States by the parties he was with when captured. I had ridden hard and was very tired and we camped on a creek in a quaking asp grove. So as to make it safe at night I handcuffed him with his arms around a tree so he could not get at the lock of the handcuffs or travel to where my arms were. I slept in peace. In the morning he was still hugging the tree. That day we went to Henry Coppic's lodge on Meadow Creek. Next day we went to Virginia City. He had a trial before the U. S. Commissioner and was acquitted on self defense. He lit out for Missouri the next day.

[August 26, 1865—unidentified newspaper item:]

Yesterday A. B. Hastings came down from where he had been working up the Gulch at Central, and sauntered into the "Exchange" and commenced playing old sledge with a friend. A man named Jake Smetzer walked in but went out again, slightly intoxicated, but appeared in a good humor. He discharged the contents of one barrel of his revolver through the end wall of the house. He went out shortly afterward but returned as Hastings and his friend were about finishing and proposed to play a game of freeze-out for a watch with Mr. Finlay. Hastings said he might as well play it off to which Smetzer replied: "If you don't take stock in it, damn you, put it down!"

Hastings said sternly to him: "Do not damn me—," upon which he jumped up—pulled his pistol and leveled it at Hastings' head. Hastings clutched the barrel as it was discharging. Smetzer fired and hit Hastings in the knee joint.

Deputy Marshal X. Beidler made swift pursuit, running his horse across the ditches, drains and sluices and caught him at the head of Bummer Dan's Gulch in a hole in the bed rock. He had re-loaded his pistol but the quick eye of X soon detected a broken cap on the new charge.

Smetzer is in jail—amputation or death are the indications from Hastings' wound. The sufferer steadfastly proclaims against the former proceeding.

Smetzer was arrested in less than 20 minutes after the commission of his crime.

[Beidler's Journal resumes:]

I jumped my horse and found Smetzer in a drift 100 feet long and not in a hole in the bed rock. I had a dark lantern and sprung it on him at the end of the drift and it blinded him. I told him if he made a move I would kill him, which he did not. Put him in jail. Hastings got well and Smetzer was acquitted.

At Virginia City in 1865, Mood and Newel[1] had opened a store and let in a man, J. E., who put in his experience against Mood and Newel's gold dust. After a very successful run of trade, they agreed to quit and follow some other business, and moved their personal effects to a new house up town, which was not yet finished. Among the effects of Mood and Newel, there was a trunk containing two sacks of gold dust of the value of $1,000. The bedding and everything was at this time supposed to be fairly divided.

J. E. knew this money was in the trunk and he came down town and told Newel that the trunk was robbed of the gold dust. Newel went and told Dr. Glick and the doctor told him to go to X. Newel did not know me, so Doc introduced him, put the case in my hands and described the gold dust and size of the nuggets.

In the meantime J. E. came to me and told me of the rob-

[1] Beidler sometimes spells this name "Newell."

110

bery and said: "We have been robbed" (claiming in on the dust).

I told J. E. to give me all the information he could in the matter. He told me there was a double door in the house which opened into the rock where the trunk was, and that the lid of the trunk had been pried open with a pick and that he would show me how it was done. This conversation was in the Shade saloon at eleven o'clock at night. J. E. asked me to stop where I was for a few minutes and he would be right back. The moon was shining and he went off on the light side of the street and I followed soon after on the dark side and watched him. He went to the house where there was a pile of shavings and I saw him stoop down and fumble around. He then came across the house and met me in front of Higgins' store, which surprised him very much as he thought I was still in the "Shade"—which I was. He asked me what I was doing there, and, to try to throw him off, I told him I heard a man snoring in a stable near by and was going to arrest him as he might have been up late the night before. He begged me not to wake up the man, and took me to the house, showed me the trunk, the marks the pick had made, and the pick itself and where it had been put.

We then went to the Shade saloon, and I asked J. E. who he suspected of the robbery. He said "Big Head" Kelly, who had worked in the store with him. I knew Kelly was innocent, but didn't say so.

Next morning I met Elk Morse, who came down with his pack train from Summit, told him of the robbery and to look out for someone who didn't work much and had plenty of money which I described. About eleven o'clock that day J. E. got up and I met him and sympathized with him over his loss and told him to rustle for the robbers. He replied by telling me to be sure and look out for Kelly. I told him about putting

Elk Morse, and that if the money went up the Gulch his way, he would get the robbers. Morse had just come in sight and I introduced him to J. E. and proposed to go to the house and look the thing over again and show Morse how the robbery was done. After J. E. had showed us through the house, we came out and sat on a log right where I had seen J. E. monkey with the shavings the evening before. While sitting there I noticed him several times throw his eyes to a particular spot and then knew I had my man. We went down street together and communed, and J. E. bid us good morning. I told Morse I would have the money in an hour.

Mood and Newel had informed the Vigilance Committee of the robbery and that it was in my hands. The Committee at this stage came and asked what luck I had had, and I told them I would report soon.

I watched around and when no one was near went to this J. E.'s anxious spot which he was looking at while we were on the log, and just under the building I pulled out the two sacks of gold dust. I then went and reported to the Vigilance Committee. The dust was poured out of the sacks and spread out, and Mood and Newel sent for to describe the dust which was easy to do as it was principally nuggets saved up for the purpose of making pins and ornaments. The dust was turned over to them by the Committee, who told Mood and Newel to pay me for my trouble.

Tom Newel was so elated over getting the dust that he rushed off and told "Big Head" Kelly, which was contrary to the orders of the Committee. They had given orders for the thing to be kept secret and for me to fill the sacks with black sand, and place them where I had found them, watch, and whenever the man came to take them away, to kill him.

Kelly went and told J. E. that the money was found and all about it, and, of course, he never came around to raise the sacks which I had to do myself. Then I was ordered to arrest J. E. and bring him before the Committee at the Adelphia Hall, Nevada. I got the hack and met J. E. and invited him to get in and ride with me, which he politely refused. I told him I couldn't go alone and that there were over a hundred nice gentlemen awaiting him at the Adelphia Hall, and they expected to receive the pleasure of his company. This made him weaken as he knew what he was wanted for and who the gentlemen were. He got into the hack sooner than have the show on the street. Before the Committee he acknowledged having stolen the money. He got a terrible reprimand from the Committee and was ordered to pay me $100, which he did and was glad to do it.

In 1865 Tom Lloyd kept a saloon in McClellan Gulch. It was a long, narrow place about fifty feet long, and had a very big fireplace at one end. Tom left Ireland early and before all his brothers had arrived from heaven. He had a brother killed at Sacramento and one at Esmeralda.

H. J. Hoppe, who was the brewer at Lincoln Gulch, met a boy who claimed to be a young brother of Tom Lloyd, but had never seen him. Hoppe and the boy went over to McClellan Gulch on snow shoes and after all hands had had a nip, Hoppe introduced the boy to Tom as one of his brothers who was born after Tom left Ireland.

Tom looked him over and said he didn't know if he was a "Lide" or not, but he would damned soon find out. He said: "Here, bie, go to the other end of the room and hould up this spoon," which the boy did.

Tom pulled out his pistol, shot and knocked the spoon out of the boy's hand, the boy never moving a muscle or saying a word. Tom rushed up to him, hugged and kissed him and swore he was "a Lide be Jasus."

X. Beidler: Vigilante

Referring to another incident of pioneer life in which his esteemed friend the Hon. J. M. Sweeney was involuntarily concerned and in this case I might say, a victim.

It was on the ninth day of June 1865 when Jno. Keene shot and killed "Slater," who was at the time in the front door of Sam Greer's saloon on Bridge St. and located just in the rear of where the International Hotel now stands; enough excitement arose and a public meeting called at once from which a jury was selected and among those chosen was Jno. M. Sweeney at that time quite young and inexperienced and in a humble manner begged to be excused from serving as a juror. Neither his age nor his eloquent pleadings availed him anything and he was about to be "sworn in" when Steve Reynolds, who was the foreman of the jury and also judge of the trial, remembered that John had the only carpenter shop in the Gulch and the only available person to construct a coffin. This important matter was sufficient evidence and John was released from serving on the jury greatly to his relief and comfort.

The jury sat until a late hour when the prisoner claimed that at Blackfoot, a distance of about 45 miles from Helena, was a witness whose testimony was vital to his cause and would unquestionably clear him. The jury then adjourned and quickly dispatched a messenger to Blackfoot for the witness; both returned at an early hour in the morning making the entire trip in really phenomenal time.

The jury convened immediately on the arrival of the witness and on a thorough examination he testified that the last time he had conversed with Keene the latter stated, "Whenever Slater and I meet one of us must die." Every opportunity was given the prisoner to establish his innocence and never was a more impartial trial held.

The jury was chosen and empaneled in the lumber yard

of Wm. Vantelburg on the precise spot where the First National Bank building now stands. Seats were made of piles of lumber and here the jurors with a unanimous verdict pronounced the death sentence of John Keene, which was heartily endorsed and accepted by the entire crowd in attendance with the possible exception of two strangers.

Mr. Vantelburg is now a resident of Gallatin County and we think residing with our friend, the Hon. Chas. Anceny.

After John had received the order for Slater's coffin he proceeded with great alacrity to take a correct measurement of "Slater," the murdered man, it then being about half past ten and became a matter of strictest diligence and rapid work to complete the coffin and resulted in his finishing it about half past five on the morning of the tenth of June.

No sooner did he have "Slater's" coffin ready than the Committee again called on John and ordered another coffin, instructing him to make it a little wider and about one inch longer than "Slater's": this duplicate order came so unexpectedly that John called his friend Jas. Aplin to assist him. Their combined efforts soon had the second coffin ready, completing it about half past ten o'clock.

Now comes the part where John was forced into a position which he says was the most difficult and trying one of his entire worldly experiences. He had just taken a short nap and was congratulating himself and thinking how fortunate he had been in obtaining his release from acting in the capacity of a juryman, when the ever vigilant Committee again paid their respects and this time notified him to prepare himself to act in the full duty as one of the guards. This announcement was a "stunner" as John had never seen a man hung and was the last person in the wide world to seek such dangling and frightful scenes; again his prayers for delivery were refused and in a moment a huge six-shooter thrust in his hand and John says when the command, "Attention!! All be ready to fire," was given, the only remarkable thing was he didn't either kill himself, or someone near him.

On the arrival of the wagon bearing the coffin with Keene seated indifferently upon it reaching Hangsman Tree in Dry Gulch at about half past eleven o'clock in the morning, Keene remarked, "He was d—— dry," and inquired if they were going to hang a thirsty man. A messenger was sent at once to the nearest saloon, returning shortly with the desired liquid. Keene took his last drink and savagely remarked "I killed the son of a b—— and would do the same thing over again and if you don't like that you can drive your d—— old cart off as fast as you d—— please."

The cart was then driven off and Keene was suspended between Heaven and Earth, there being no drop to the rope, and in about twenty-three minutes and after several convulsive struggles he was pronounced dead.

Uncle Johnny Thorburn who still resides in Helena buried both Keene and Slater. Thus terminated the result of the first criminal trial ever held in Last Chance Gulch where the attractive and energetic city of Helena now stands.

[IX]

Indian Captive

I WAS COLLECTOR of customs under Andrew Johnson, for Montana and Idaho. My bondsmen for $10,000 were John Kinna and W. A. Rumsey, both of Helena.[1]

I was instructed to rent an office for which I paid $100 per month, furnished by the government.

The first collector appointed, but he didn't qualify, was General Connors and I was then appointed in his stead. At that time there was no boundary survey and we didn't know where the line between Canadian and United States territory was; consequently, there were no customs to collect. We didn't know where people came from. After trying to get posted and to find out where and who to collect from, I was informed that goods were being smuggled from the British possessions into the United States.

Then there was not a settlement or house built north of Fort Benton, or a single white habitation. The country was full of Bloods, Blackfeet, Piegans, and buffalo.

At Fort Benton I met Major Culbertson and informed him that I had to go north on official business. He said he would go with me. We hitched up two teams, one two-horse and one four-horse team and went to I. G. Baker's store and loaded up with Indian goods for trade. Culbertson was mar-

[1] Included with the longhand manuscript is also a newspaper clipping, with the penciled notation, *"Courier,* December 30, 1886." The article, almost word for word like this chapter, is entitled: "In 1867 X. Beidler's Captivity Among the Blood's and Blackfeet. A Chapter of Perilous Incidents for X. Beidler's Forthcoming Book."

ried to a Blood Indian woman. Gov. Stevens, who had seen her, claimed her to be a peerless woman, and she was, in her day, in that Indian country.

After Culbertson had outfitted with what he wanted to take, I went and put some flour, tobacco, needles, thread, looking glasses, etc., into the wagons to give to the Indians. Culbertson and his wife, knowing the country so well, I was governed by them for camping places. We traveled and camped and camped and traveled, making 15 to 20 miles a day, and nothing of interest occurred until we got to Belly River. While there was no boundary line, we didn't know exactly where we were, and simply had to guess at it.

Culbertson told me we were on the British side, in his judgment. While we were in camp, we discovered a band of horses grazing on the prairie, and I remarked that they were too big for Indian horses. We soon discovered that there was a soldiers' camp above us, which turned out to be in command of Lieut. Hogan, with one company of cavalry from Fort Shaw. Having met him before, he was pleased to see me; asked me where I was going, etc.; told him I was collector of customs and didn't know exactly where I was going. I asked him what he was doing there. He said he had some citizens with him looking for horses stolen from them from Lincoln and McClellan gulches, on the Western slope. I said: "Lieutenant, do you know that you are across the line with U. S. troops?"

He appeared surprised, and said: "My guide, Veial, didn't tell me so."

I told him Veial didn't know and he said that he would have to return. I found in his camp Joe Campbell, from Lincoln, and Frank Galmich, from the Dearborn. So when Lieut. Hogan agreed to go back, Campbell, Galmich, S. Robair, and Cut-Lip Jack agreed to go north with me; we crossed Belly River and went north about two days and went into camp. Culbertson decided not to go any further but to stay there, where about thirty lodges were also camped and he could sell out his goods to them. At the same time I was assisting Campbell and Galmich to secure their horses. The Indians had stolen a lot of mules from Wells, Fargo on the Benton route and I was also looking for them. We left the Culbertson camp about 10 A. M., and before I left Culbertson gave me a letter to Jean LaRue, Indian priest. Next day we went north and in the evening we got in sight of a band of 300 lodges of Indians on the banks of the Saskatchewan River,—a splendid camp with the finest grass and timber ever mortal eyes looked upon.

The Indian drums were beating all night; even the buffalo wanted to hover near this camp—it was so beautiful. The Indians were in their glory, and well they might be.

We had been riding by two or three bands of horses, slick and fat, belonging to this camp, when S. T. Robair stopped and said: "What do you want up in this country?"

I told him I was collector of customs and wanted to find out who was smuggling goods into the U. S., and that I was looking also for stolen horses.

He said: "You are out of the U. S., and why shouldn't we take and drive a thousand or two of these fine horses back home over the line; we shall then be even and ahead, and no one to bother us."

I did not agree with him, as I told him I did not come to steal horses.

"Well," says he, "what will you do?"

I told him I had a letter from Maj. Culbertson to Jean LaRue, an Indian priest in the camp.

119

X. Beidler: Vigilante

"Well," says he, "if we go into that camp we must go in at peep of day, for, if they catch us on the prairie, they will kill us. After we get into the camp we are all right."

We got on our horses and rode into camp just at daybreak. Like all Indian camps, the old men were out straggling around, and they halloed in Indian that the white men were coming. "Nopecums coming."

One Indian sent the word to another and he to the next and so on, so quick that it would make a telephone ashamed of itself. When we got into camp there was not a lodge that there was not from one to four Indians, armed to the teeth, at the door. I wanted to find where this priest I had the letter for lived, and Robair, who could talk good Blackfoot, enquired for us. They directed us from one place to another and after two hours search we found him in an Indian lodge. He came out of the door with a long gown on him,—so slick and greasy that if a fly had lit on him it could not have stayed—and with a chain and big cross around his neck. S. T. Robair said: "That's the man you want to see."

I reached out my hand and said: "Father LaRue, I have a letter from Maj. Culbertson I wish to show you."

He shook hands with Cut-Lip Jack and Robair,—he knew them before. I then introduced him to Joe Campbell and Galmich and told him they came with me. The priest spoke good English and shook hands.

I handed him the letter and said: "Father, in addition, I have some of the latest papers to give you," knowing news was scarce.

He thanked me very kindly and appeared to be the most affable gentleman I had ever met. In this letter Culbertson stated who I was and what my business was—looking for horses, mules and smugglers, and where the property belonged.

I said: "Father, I don't understand the Blackfoot language, and if you will be kind enough to tell these Indians what I want, I will take the property and leave your camp."

He got up and stood on an elevation and read the letter to the Indians in the Indian language, and what interpretation he put on it I never knew; but in thirty minutes from the time he commenced to read that letter there was not a lodge standing out of the 300. The Indians were all working, packing up, taking down tepees, fetching in horses, etc., etc., and talking all the time. It seemed as if they had all gone wild. Campbell, Galmich, and myself were taken prisoners.

They moved camp about 8 or 10 miles to a lake, where the squaws were ahead to put up the camp and we were guarded by 20 Indians, but we would not give up our arms, which they wanted. When we came to camp in the evening the lodges were up and we were conducted to the soldier lodge. The Indians ran races all day on the road for strings of beads and such things. While in the lodge I asked for some water to drink, and an Indian who had just washed himself and his hair in a basin of water, handed this same water to me to drink, which I had to do, because it was just as good, if not better, than the water I would have got if I had gone after some myself. (J. J. Healy, now in Alaska, claims the Indians forced me to drink a Blackfoot cocktail, which is only a little fun on his part.) We were fed on meat straight during our captivity, but it was good and fat, and I had a small sack of salt with me, which helped me greatly, and my friends, Campbell and Galmich, begged and begged, but I kept it all myself, and I guess they growl at me to this day for not giving them a few pinches of salt for their straight meat; the Indians wanted to know what it was and I told them it was bad "medicine."

These Indians kept us with them, under guard, from one buffalo camp to another; staying from one to three days in each, and by way of a little diversion threatened to kill us several times, but treated us better as we became better acquainted. The priest never showed up again to us after reading that letter to the Indians. I asked for him and got the Indians to go after him, but he said the Indians were angry at us and he couldn't do us any good.

During our conversations, while in captivity with the Indians, Cut-Lip and S. T. Robair told the Indians about the soldiers we left on Belly River, and when they heard that and that those soldiers were guides of ours, and other lies, the Indians got terrible mad as they did not appear to get a right version of the matters. Extra look-outs were put on and a great excitement prevailed all the time in the camp and if a soldier had been in sight, they (the Indians) certainly would have killed us. The Indians took care of my horse and I kept my saddle and pistols in the guard tepee with me. One day, one of the soldier Indians, who was guarding me, told me that an Indian was riding my horse and showed me the circus—a young buck, covered with beads and paint, was putting my horse through for all he was worth. I stepped outside with my six-shooter on and made a sign for him to get off. I caught hold of the lariat and stopped the horse, and, catching the Indian by the foot, I threw him off the horse, on the opposite side. I knew I might as well die there as to be set afoot in that country. The Indian got up and made a big talk, and a large crowd of Indians gathered around and those Indians who saw the fracas, my throwing the Indian off the horse, etc., laughed at the Indian and called him a squaw. I then asked the Indian what he was going to do about it, now, that the white man had taken the horse from him. Robair (interpreter) came up and wanted to know what was the matter. I told him I didn't want to steal a horse to go home on and couldn't walk (being lame). Robair said that the Indians were talking of killing me, which, of course, I couldn't help. I told Robair to tell the Indians that I would fight any one of the tribe right there, and that we would step out and shoot until one of us went over. This made me some very good friends, while it made others more bitter against me. Not an Indian took me up on my proposition. Robair told me that if I did step out I would be killed, sure, as I couldn't win anyway; but I had it in my head that I might as well take my "medicine" in public, as in private.

"Bullsback Fat,"[2] an Indian and principal chief of the Blood tribe, was present. He was a brother-in-law of Culbertson, from whom I had received the letter to the priest. Robair told him what I had done and why I was prisoner; also told him what Culbertson had said in the letter to the priest. This Indian, "Bullsback Fat," stepped out and talked very strong to the Indians; told them I was his relative's friend; that I had offered to fight, if that was what they wanted, and that they ought to be ashamed of themselves, etc. This talk had a very favorable effect for me and the worst growlers stuck their tails between their legs and skulked off to their tepees. This quieted things down some. Robair told me it was a very scaley time for me once, as he had heard them agree to kill me, right there.

After this everything went on smoothly for several days, —as pleasant as I could expect. The little bucks, however, would insult me at every chance, which I had to put up with. When I got tired of being a prisoner I told Robair I wanted to get out. They seemed to take more care in keeping me than they did Campbell and Galmich; they knocked around the camp and did as they pleased, but the Indians seemed down on me because I was reported to be an officer and with the soldiers from the American side. I sent Robair to tell the

2 Beidler sometimes spells this name "Bull's back-fat."

chiefs of the camp to get together and have a council; that I had made up my mind to go and they had to let me leave the Indians and go home. They held a pow-wow—over a thousand of them. I was having a trial and got S. T. Robair to explain to them, while in council, that it was an accident I had been with the soldiers, and how I came to be with them, and, in fact, everything concerning me. Many of the Indians hollered out that it was a lie; that I was a fox and that if I escaped I would return with the soldiers and scare the buffalo away and give them trouble. After a very long parley they agreed to let me go with the understanding that 12 chiefs,— 4 Bloods, 4 Piegans, and 4 Blackfeet—should go with me to the line and see that I should not be molested. These Indians at once wanted to know how much pay they would get for escorting me to the line. I told them I had nothing, but if I could get them to Benton I would give them a lot of blankets and grub. It was finally agreed who should go. "Bullsback Fat" was one designated to go with me, and another one,— the best I ever saw—his name was "The Passing Cloud." I afterwards named him "Now-you-see-him-and-now-you-don't." About all the Indians were afraid of him. He was a great fighter.

Campbell, Galmich, and myself were placed in the center of these escorts of ours, and when about to start we could see Indians coming around from different directions. They did not want us to get away. Robair and Cut-Lip Jack helped us when we started and Cut-Lip must have knocked over not less than a dozen Indians, and our guards could not get through the crowd of dissatisfied Indians and we had to have another pow-wow, which we had right there.

"White Swan," who was bitterly against me, got up and said: "I have heard you are an officer on the American side. You may be a big chief when at home, but you are not there."

He reached down to the ground and picked up a little piece of dirt and rubbed it between his thumb and finger and said: "You are like this piece of dirt over here and I think as much of you as I do of it." He crumbled it and let it drop to the ground and said, "You are on our Grandmother's ground [meaning the Queen's]. You whites have killed us Indians every time you have had a chance; why should we not kill you?" and, addressing the Indians, continued, "Let us kill these 'Nanpaquins' [white men]. We have a good chance. They would kill us." I supposed my curly locks were about to ornament some buck's girdle.

The twelve guards held the balance as level as they could. Robair and Cut-Lip Jack came into the center with us and stayed with us, and there was so much talk that I couldn't understand, that I asked Robair who said, "You may be damned glad you don't know." I said I wanted to know. He said, "Well, they say they will kill you." Campbell threw a cartridge into his gun and I hollered don't shoot or we will all go to hell, sure.

Robair, right at this moment, rushed out of the center and said: "Look at that Sun. [Indians are superstitious.] If you kill that white man you will never see that Sun again." It had its effect. He hollered very loud when he drew their attention to the sun. They all heard him—he talked long and loud in reference to the sun and me, and it made a stampede among them, and some of them commenced to holler and sing and the dogs commenced to howl and the squaws to cry, and the 12 chiefs commenced to sing a plaintive, doleful song.

During all this time, and just before this racket quit, an Indian came in and brought two mules that had been stolen from Wells, Fargo & Co. We started and had got out about half a mile and they again came after us. It appears that Galmich, while in camp, had traded off some blankets he had

125

to an Indian for a horse which he was riding. They came and took his horse, saddle and bridle away from him, after having had possession of it 2 weeks, and he didn't get his blankets either so he had to ride one of the mules bare-back. A whole gang of young bucks and others followed us and Cut-Lip Jack was fighting them all the time with a club. He was very rough with them and I expected to hear a gun go off at any moment, and I knew that such an event would have settled our business.

While we were skirmishing along, all at once our guards hollered "Mush-ter poot," which means Go, and there was a little knob or butte of land ahead of us. The Indians pointed to it and signalled us to go and hide there as there was another band of Indians coming from behind, and we had scarcely got to the other side of this butte when a party of 40 or 50 Indians were coming from the other way and rushing towards us. Old Bullsback Fat hollered to us to come back quick as soon as he saw them, which we did, and got inside their lines. Then we made about a five-mile run from them as fast as we could make our animals go, and we left them. Some of them got off their horses and watched us, and others went back.

We traveled till night, when we struck some good water and camped for two hours, picketed our horses, and went to eating our dried meat, as usual. We traveled that night and camped in the morning close to a lake, very tired, where we stayed only until a little after daylight, when I was awakened by the report of a gun, and found that "Now-you-see-him-and-now-you-don't" had killed a nice fat buffalo cow, which, of course, means a feast, and you ought to have seen us going for that meat. We were tired, hungry, away from the enemy, and we roasted ribs to our heart's content. As soon as we had filled up we started again and traveled until evening, and during the trip, about noon, "Now-you-see-him" killed another buffalo, cut it up, and put it in a couple of feet of water in a lake close by, intending to take it on his way back. This is a very good plan to keep meat in that country, as there are no trees—only sage brush and buffalo chips.

That evening we got to Maj. Culbertson's camp. Here I gave the Indians a feast—sugar, coffee, tea, tobacco, etc., and a general fill up, and each one a little something to take back home.

Frank Galmich, Campbell, and myself left there next morning for the crossing of Sun River, and there was nothing of interest after this until we arrived at Sun River at Largent & Hamilton's store, turned the mules over to Wells, Fargo & Co.'s agent. Galmich went to the Dearborn, where he lived; Campbell went to McClellan Gulch mines and I remained at Sun River three or four days to get rested up—glad to be alive—and from there went to Helena, my home and old stamping ground, if I had any on this mundane sphere.

[X]

Scattered Adventures

WHILE at Virginia City in the summer of 1866, a man came in on the Salt Lake road and reported that road agents had held up a party and killed one man by the name of Blodgett. I was ordered by the Vigilance Committee to go and take in the situation. I was told to take a good man with me. It did not take me long to find a man to fill the bill. I called on Bill Deacy, a Frenchman from Cork—I don't mean corkscrew, I ain't mean enough.

We saddled up and rode about 40 miles to Black Tail Creek and camped about midnight. We turned our horses loose with picket ropes but did not picket. A stranger could not get to our horses if they were not picketed, so we took our chances that the horses would not run away. They were tired as well as ourselves. We had no bedding, only our saddle blankets. We were under the foot of the main Rocky Mountain range. It was cold. I told Bill it would not do to build a fire,—that it would give us away. I looked around and found an old rawhide that had been left by some party. I told Bill we could put that under us and cover with the saddle blankets. He was pleased and piled into bed while I had to spread the blankets. Bill took the middle of the rawhide bed. I asked him which side of the bed I should take. He said both sides, that he had the middle. As it happened after we had gone to our little bed, my friend had fallen into the sleep of the innocents and snored like a band of Mormon wives. It then commenced to rain and I crawled out and let my friend have his sleep. I didn't forget to take the blankets with me. I made camp under a pine tree. Shelter under the tallest pine of the forest! Daylight came as usual. I woke up and looked down at my friend. He was camping in three inches of good, cold, rain water. He had a good bath for the first time since his horse threw him in the Big Hole, or Wisdom River, as Lewis and Clark named it in 1804. We got our horses, saddled up and went to the scene of the murder. Bill was drying his clothes on the willows. He is a nice boy.

We went to Sage Creek across the range and overtook the train. We arrested Taylor. He had the Blodgett span of mules that Blodgett had paid $500 for. He also had charge of the Blodgett train. I told Taylor to order the train into the station. It was kept by Johnson. I said to Taylor that the train would be subject to my order.

Taylor kicked and the Mormons said to Taylor that he needn't go unless he wanted to, intimating that they would keep him from me. I told them they did not know what they were talking about. I told Bill Deacy to ride ahead of the train and order a halt, at the same time telling Taylor he was my prisoner, and to turn the train and go into corral. I told Taylor we were going back to investigate the death of Blodgett. This was about 10 A.M. After corralling the train and making everything secure, Deacy and I with the prisoner, Taylor, started back to Virginia City. Deacy and the prisoner rode in the wagon and I rode horseback. Sometimes I would change off with Deacy and during our ride and when we got to the place where Blodgett was killed, Taylor explained how he got possession of the mules. He said he purchased the mules from Blodgett for $500, paying him in gold dust in the night. I wanted to know how he could pay in gold dust that night as it was as black as ink and he couldn't see. He could not answer. He then told me that Blodgett got killed by road agents coming and catching Blodgett unawares while he was sitting under the wagon tongue making tongue stiffeners and for proof showed me the chips where he had been making the stiffeners, then showed me the trail of the road agents where they had run after killing Blodgett. I went and looked at the road agents' trail and found the tracks were all made by the same sized boots and that they were the same exactly as Taylor's. I told him these road agents all wore the same sized boots.

On our way to hunt for Taylor we went by Blodgett's grave. There we found a pocket knife where he had been pulled out of the wagon before burial, which had fallen out of Blodgett's pocket. I put it in my pocket and kept it. A man told us nearby that Taylor buried Blodgett without a coffin or change of clothes, while there were plenty of good clothes of Blodgett's on the wagon.

When I got through near where Blodgett was killed, I went through Taylor and found $500 in gold dust in each of Taylor's boots which I took care of. We then started again for Virginia City to make a night run and just before dark a jack rabbit jumped up in front of the team and I whistled at it and it stopped. I shot at it and killed it and Taylor hurried around and said he hoped I should never shoot at him and seemed scared. I told him I hoped not to have to but that if I did I would knock him out.

We got into Virginia City before daylight with our prisoner and went to a restaurant and had rabbit for breakfast and turned our prisoner over to the Vigilance Committee. I also turned over the $1,000 in dust which I had taken from Taylor to Col. Demling of Virginia City. Worn out and tired, Deacy and I retired. While no one except Taylor witnessed the murder of Blodgett, the Vigilance Committee acquitted him.

Next morning I was instructed to get the $1,000 and turn

them and the team over to Taylor. I obeyed orders and gave him an order on Johnson for his train. And I will here state that there was never a more heinous, cold blooded murder committed in Montana than this, and the proprietor [perpetrator?] went scott free.

Blodgett had a wife and family at Ogden waiting for his return, expecting to get the gold dust upon his arrival, but Taylor, a brother Mormon, never gave them a cent and left them in destitute circumstances, himself being rich at the time.

Taylor, when explaining his story to the Committee, told them that Mr. Blodgett had purchased a pocket knife for one of his children and was taking it home but the road agents even took that out of his pocket and that he saw them do it. I stepped up and asked Taylor if he would know the pocket knife if he saw it. He said he would. I then showed it to him. He asked, surprised, where I got it and I told him from the road agents.

Taylor went home to enjoy his plunder and I went on the road as messenger again, and Sheriff Brown of Box Elder Co., at Ogden, came to me one day, knowing me, and told me that Taylor was going to have me killed. I met Taylor one day and I told him what I had heard and also told him that he would never have a better chance than right then; that he was a murderer and I knew it; that he not only killed the husband and robbed him but also robbed the family of their money and property and that if I ever heard any more noise from him I would kill him.

He said: "I will quit."

I said: "You have got to." I have never seen him since.

I took special interest in this murder as Blodgett's brother lives in Bitter Root Valley and Taylor is still in Utah.

The *Montana Post,* September 2, 1866, published this item:

X. Beidler: Vigilante

ROAD AGENTS

On Monday last, about 9 A.M., Messrs. Taylor and Blodgett were travelling on their way to Salt Lake, about 25 miles from Virginia City in Cedar Cañon, when they were attacked by four men on foot with blackened faces. Blodgett was killed at sight, two balls striking him on the back of the head and one in the shoulder.

His partner made his escape and sent word to his father, a man by the name of Taylor who lives in Nevada, he himself after burying the body—which he hauled to Price's ranch some 20 miles farther on—made quick time for Salt Lake City.

The Vigilance Committee with a promptness that did them great credit, at once overhauled Mr. Taylor, the sole witness of the affair, and as we hear, made a thorough investigation of the case. Mr. Taylor is now on his way to Salt Lake.[1]

Confederate Gulch in Meagher County was one of the richest placer camps in the world and considerable treasure was shipped from there to Helena. Two tons and a quarter of gold dust, valued at about $900,000, was shipped from Diamond City in Confederate Gulch to Helena in the fall of 1866 and placed in Hershfield's bank.

I was in Diamond City a couple of weeks previous to this shipment and Mr. Fredericks asked me if I could be employed to guard this money from Helena to Fort Benton, to which place they had concluded to ship it and then load it on a steamboat for the States. I agreed to go along. He didn't know exactly the time he would start, but told me to consider myself employed and to keep a lookout for the toughs in the meantime.

[1] Only a longhand transcription of this article appears in the Beidler journals. The date given there is 1865, which is obviously wrong since the killing of Blodgett took place in 1866.

JOHN X. BEIDLER
BORN AUG. 14, 1831
DIED JAN. 22, 1890
3 - 7 - 77
PUBLIC BENEFACTOR
BRAVE PIONEER
TO TRUE OCCASION TRUE
ERECTED BY THE
SOCIETY OF MONTANA PIONEERS.

Montana State Historical Society

Memorial plaque on Beidler's gravestone,
Helena, Montana

X. Beidler: Vigilante

Mr. Fredericks in the winter of 1861 was out prospecting in Colorado near the Gunnison country and was snowed in for the winter and had to eat his pack animals to sustain life. I met him in the spring as he was coming out near the Twin Lakes. He came to my camp nearly starved to death. I fed him and his party some good, substantial grub which they had not seen for six months. Mr. Fredericks never forgot that square meal and the next I saw of him was at Diamond City where he employed me. He brought out a pan of dust and set it on the table and said: "X, help yourself to a nugget."

I picked out a pretty one that weighed $42.

He said: "X, there are larger pieces there—take a big one." Several weighed over 3 or 4 hundred dollars, but I was too delicate and kept the $42 one. Always was foolish.

We started from Helena to Benton with the dust loaded on 3 two-mule wagons,—the dust in 3 little safes, and fourteen men armed and a-horseback. Job Travis went along to bring the horses back.

While in the bank on Bridget St., Helena, getting the money ready, one of the Germans interested in the money let his double-barreled shotgun go off accidentally and the charge went into the ceiling which raised quite a commotion.

We started after being fully prepared for almost any emergency and camped in Prickly Pear Cañon that night. While in camp a man came to me—an outsider who was posted about the treasure and asked me if he would whistle would I whistle back. Then he would come and have the treasure taken off and I should get my whack. He started in to tell me his plans —telling me I was to fix the guns so that they could be stolen also, and that then there would be no killing done on either side. I told him I didn't want to hear any more plans. I knew the man and was and am very well acquainted with him. I told him if he whistled I would kill him if I could.

I reported the proposition to Fredericks and it alarmed the outfit and we put on a heavy guard—2 hours on guard and 2 off. No whistling and no money taken. Next night we camped at the Dearborn. Had no trouble until we got to Bull's Head, twelve miles this side of Benton. While riding at a walk my riding animal broke his right forward leg just below the knee, through no apparent cause—no gopher hole, rock or anything to cause it—and how it was done no one of us could find out. It just snapped off. We shot him right there and left him and I rode on in the wagon to Benton.

While we were there we fixed the safes ready for shipping down the river by Macman, no steamboat being there. We fastened empty 10-gallon kegs with ropes to each safe in case of accident and upset, for buoys, to find where the safes were if swamped.

I got 11 ounces for my trip. The safes got through to the States all right.

At Helena, Montana, in 1866, Christmas turkey was Christmas turkey and we had to depend upon our good Mormon brethren 600 miles south of us over snow covered mountains, almost impassable, for our Christmas turkey bird. We did not then know that one of our good old grangers had reared 100 fine young turkeys in the Prickly Pear Valley for us honest miners, but he did and brought them in for sale at the snug little sum of $25 in gold dust each. They went off as fast as he could weigh out the dust. He sold the 100 turkeys and I supposed he was happy but he was not. I met him later. He was sitting on a log near where his horses were feeding, his head bowed down and apparently in great trouble. I approached him and asked him if anything serious was the matter. He asked me to please go away and let him alone, which I did.

X. Beidler: Vigilante

"The whites have gone crazy! The whites have gone crazy!" These were the words the Piegan Indian known as "Two Wolves" told his tribe when he arrived home after escaping from William Hamilton and myself at Helena while attending the Theater.

In 1866 "Two Wolves," a witness in a U. S. case against some parties for selling whiskey to Indians, was brought to Helena and in charge of Bill Hamilton, deputy marshal under G. M. Pinney. I was also a deputy, and the Marshal and Deputies all wanted to go to the Theater. If we all went we had to take the Indian with us or we might lose him.

We went to the Jack Langrishe Theater and during the tragedy the actors got to killing one another in great shape. The Indian got scared, thinking everything was in earnest, jumped up, fired himself through the window onto the porch and down to the ground when he lit out like a streak of lightning. The first horse he ran across was his. Right quick he rode bareback to Clark's ranche in Prickly Pear Cañon where he stole a good saddle and nothing was heard again from or of him until I met him in the Piegan Camp, when he asked me if the whites were still killing one another and laughing at it. I think he still believes the killing was in reality. The whiskey case went over for want of the prosecuting witness.

Bill Hamilton, besides being Deputy Marshal, was Sheriff of Choteau County and when he had lost his Indian, issued the following proclamation, which he had posted on every prominent tree and place between Helena and Benton:

PROCLAMATION

Hi, William Hamilton, eye Sheriff hof Choteau County, hand Deputy Hunited States Marshal horder hall men to arrest one Hindian named "Two Wolves" hand bring im himmediately to my hoffice dead or halive to Fort Benton.

Signed   Serenely yours
Wm. Hamilton

Witnessed by Robt. Hereford.

[*From an unidentified newspaper clipping:*][2]

One of the most noted Indian fighters of the frontier is Liver-Eating Johnson. At present he is past the prime but of magnificent physique and yet able and willing to take a hand with anyone white or red—who wishes to collide with him. A sailor by occupation, he came from the coast about thirty years ago, and being exceptionally expert with his gun he was known as a bad man to impose upon. He followed wolf hunting and trapping with a big sprinkling of Indian fighting for over twenty years and the adventures and hair-breadth escapes of this man would fill a large volume. No man of the frontier is much better known than "Liver-Eating." The manner in which he gained his name is as follows:

At the mouth of the Musselshell River, in the summer of 1866, Capt. Hawley kept a trading post and quite a number of wolfers stopped at his place, doing nothing in the summer time.

One day in July, Mrs. Jennie Hawley, accompanied by a friendly squaw, belonging to one of the wolfers, were about three hundred yards from the trading post, engaged in picking berries. While busy filling their baskets, they were fired upon by Sioux Indians concealed in the brush. Mrs. Hawley fell, shot through the neck, and the squaw through the fleshy portion of her anatomy, but she was able to skip for the post, yelling at every jump. The wolfers responded quickly, but

[2] The heading of this newspaper article says, "Extract from J. X. Beidler's Coming Book."

before they could reach the scene of the shooting, the noble sons of the prairie had relieved Mrs. Hawley of her scalp. On examination of her wound, it was found she was only creased, the bullet striking the chords of her neck, merely stunning her. Water dashed in her face soon restored her and she was assisted to the house, while a party of wolfers consisting of Johnson, Geo. Grinell, Jim Dees, and seven others, whose names have slipped my memory, went after the Indians.

The savages kept on the outside of the timber for about half a mile and then dropped into a washout on the river bank, intending to ambush the boys. Johnson's quick eye detected the ruse and the wolfers came down through the willows, and appeared close to the willows, so close, in fact, that the Indians dared not look out and the boys dared not look in.

The washout was about thirty yards long, ten yards wide, and about ten feet deep. The Indians would raise up their cue [coup] sticks and the boys would amuse themselves by shooting them in two. Various plans were devised for ousting the Indians from their stronghold. About sundown two of the boys went around to the mouth of the washout which they found barricaded with shields made from the necks of buffalo bulls; blankets were also hung up to keep the whites from taking aim. The two men being armed with Spencer rifles (at that time being considered a splendid arm) opened fire and the shields and blankets offering no resistance, the balls went whistling through. The Indians immediately commenced to sing their death song and climb out over the walls of the washout. It offered a splendid chance for the boys to avenge the injury to Mrs. Hawley. Thirty-two of the savages passed in their checks in nearly as many seconds. One of the Indians was shot through both hips and was sitting up. Jimmy Dees approached him, and drawing his revolver (a cap and ball affair) held it close to the Indian's head and snapped the cap, which being wet the revolver could not be discharged. The Indian winked, but finding himself still alive, pleaded for his life. He was informed that he was too good to live in this wicked world and that his home was in Heaven. After snapping the remaining five caps, with the usual amount of dodging, winking, and pleading by the Indian, Johnson stepped up and claimed him as his Injun, and putting his rifle close to his head blew his brains out. The boys then quartered the dead Indians and piled them up in one large pile, reserving the heads, scalps, and trinkets. Johnson picked up the liver of an Indian and holding it up asked: "Who will take some liver rare?"

Several ran up and Johnson devoured about half a liver; the other boys backed down and from that he got the name of Liver-Eating Johnson.

The heads of the Indians were taken to the post and the flesh boiled off, then the skulls were placed on a platform and labeled. They proved a great curiosity to the people aboard the steamboats plying between St. Louis and Fort Benton.

Mrs. Hawley survived the shock and is yet living, but wears a wig. Johnson is still living near Billings and bids fair to outlive many a younger man.

[XI]

Johnny Bull

AT THE TIME that the first circus appeared in Helena, all the boys—young and old—were hungry for the circus, and my chums and running mates all being together one evening, we concluded to shake the dice to see who should buy the tickets for the crowd. I got stuck. Admittance was $2.00, and I recollect it took 2 oz. of dust to settle the bill. At that time everybody carried a buckskin with gold dust and it generally had considerable sand in the sack towards the bottom end of the dust as the merchants etc., used to take out the gold as they were paid for anything and blow back the sand—and it happened that when I went to settle for our circus tickets, it was towards the tail end of my gold dust and the ticket seller remarked: "Partner, there is considerable sand here."

"Yes, I said, "but you don't remark anything about the gold dust that's there."

He shoveled it in and gave me my tickets.

After we had taken in the circus, we all went down town and naturally fell into the John Ming Saloon, and Len Robinson, who was the concoctor, learning that we had been to the circus, asked me if we had seen Johnny Bull yet. I didn't understand him and asked him what he meant, his look attracting my attention. I said: "What's the matter?"

He said: "Johnny Bull has killed Farmer Peale."[1]

I asked him if he was in earnest as Peale was such a rattler that I didn't think he would be killed.

[1] Beidler sometimes spells this name "Peal."

I immediately went up town and found Farmer Peale dead. The officers, Howie, Featherstone,[2] and Bob Hereford were all anxiously looking for Bull, who had killed Peale. I learned from a friend that Bull kept his horse in Monte's stable at the head of Main Street, Helena. I approached Monte who was standing in the stable door and I said: "Monte, how did you like the circus?"

I was giving him the circus talk and walking through the stable at the time and looking out for Bull's horse, and I saw a horse in a stall with a saddle on (this was after 11 o'clock at night). Before going to the stable I saw a solid friend of mine and told him to get a half dozen men immediately and surround the stable and not allow any horse to leave the stable without my consent.

Then I told Monte: "That's Bull's horse."

He admitted it and I told him I must have Bull and he then asked me to wait 10 minutes and not leave the stable. He left and I followed him close up. He went into a house and hadn't been in a minute before I came up to the door and demanded admission and I was told to wait.

I said "No."

In went the door from outside pressure—there stood Bull and Monte talking.

I stepped up to Bull and told him to come with me. He wanted to know if I was going to hang him. I said: "No, sir. I will put you in gaol and give you a hearing."

I held my pistol on him during this time and asked him to take off his belt, pistol and knife which he had on, and lay it on the table. I then ordered Monte to put on the belt and pistol and told Bull not to be alarmed as I was going to take him to the Marshal's by the back road, because if I had taken

[2] Beidler refers to him variously as "Featherston," "Fetherstun," and "Featherstone."

him down Main St. his friends would have rescued him—or his enemies would have hung him.

We reached the office and Bull was happy, being afraid of the Vigilantes. I told Monte to take off his belt and pistol and put it in the drawer in the corner of the room and to go up town and tell Neil Howie to come at once to the Marshal's office and come with him and not to let anyone know about the capture.

Howie and Monte came to the office and I introduced Howie to Bull as the man who had killed Farmer Peale. Howie was much surprised to see the murderer captured and I told Howie that I had promised Mr. Bull that he should be tried by the court and that we must protect him. Howie took Bull by the hand and said: "What X said goes and we will protect you."

That took another little load off of Bull's heart.

Howie, Bull, Monte, and myself went and put him in the County Jail and afterwards we strolled up town and great crowds of men were congregated at street crossings and corners discussing the situation. We were asked several times by Peale's friends why we didn't go and rustle to get the prisoner—that we ought to go and get Bull and not let him escape—while Bull's friends said that if we found him we couldn't arrest him. Their imprecations were heaped upon us by both sides thick and fast and almost beyond human endurance, and I finally got tired and told them to go down to the County Jail and talk to him if they wanted to through the bars. There was a rush to the jail by Bull's enemies and friends to find out the truth of my statement and Featherstone, who was jailer, seeing a big crowd coming, thought it must be either the Vigilantes to hang Bull or his friends to release him, and got his buck-shot gun and very forcibly ordered the crowd to halt and wanted to know their business. They said: "Is Bull in jail?"

Montana State Historical Society

X. Beidler, Vigilante

He said: "Yes, and you can't have him."

Again they asked the question, not believing he had been captured. They then asked if they could see him, and were told, "Not tonight." This did not satisfy the crowd so Featherstone proposed that two of them should step forward and then they could look for themselves through the bars, and satisfy the balance. Featherstone saying he could stand two of them off. The 2 men walked forward covered by Featherstone's shotgun to the bars. One of them was a Peale man and the other a Bull man. Bull talked with them and convinced them that he was inside and the crowd dispersed, thoroughly satisfied that Bull was in safe keeping and that the officers had done their duty. Bull soon after had his trial and was acquitted.

In 1882, after thinking J. C. Bull to have been dead a number of years, I read the following in the *Independent:*[3]

Yesterday while the editor was busy in the supervision of his Sunday paper, he was interrupted by the entrance of a gentlemanly looking stranger who enquired if he was in.

"Do you not know me?" asked the stranger, pulling off his hat.

A long and searching glance followed the query but we could not recall ever having seen the man before, and felt satisfied, had we done so, we should not have forgotten it.

"My name is Bull—John C. Bull," he said, "the man you successfully defended fifteen years ago for killing Langford Peale."

Another glance satisfied us that the stranger was none other than an old client who in conjunction with W. Y. Pemberton, now of Butte, we defended in 1867.

His brow had become furrowed, his heavy beard and hair

[3] This story is part of the longhand manuscript. No clipping is included in the Beidler journals.

streaked with gray, but in his eye there still shone the same look of desperate courage which had so impressed us years ago when a mere boy he had startled the Territory by meeting, in mortal combat, and overcoming the most desperate desperado of the mountains, Langford Peale. Peale had killed some seven or eight men. He could fire at the drop of the hat, and hit a dollar ten paces every time. He was consequently cock of the walk in early days in Helena, and no one dared to dispute his supremacy. He had become unfriendly with Bull for some cause, and meeting him one evening in Greer's saloon, a large hall upon Main St., slapped him in the face. Bull at once resented the insult by defying him, but told him he was not armed.

"But," he said, fixing his gaze on the desperado, "you cannot make a mark that I will not come to."

"Go then, damn you," answered Peale, "and heel yourself."

"I go," said Bull, "but I will come back again."

"Come fighting," sneered the desperado, as his boyish looking antagonist turned and left the saloon. And Bull did return.

Hastily arming himself and giving directions as to his property, in the event of his death, leaving also tender messages for his mother and other members of his family, he then returned to Greer's saloon.

He had been gone about an hour. Peale had watched the door for his return, but as the moments sped, he felt sure that his foe dared not face him, and turning to his mistress, who was a faro dealer in the saloon, proposed that they retire for the night, as it was after eleven o'clock. Offering her his arm, they started for the door, and had just emerged from it to the sidewalk when they met Bull face to face.

"There he is, Langford," cried the woman, clutching his arm. The desperate men both were quick as lightning. But the woman, holding the arm of Peale, placed him at a disadvantage, and before he could fire, Bull's unerring bullet had crushed through Peale's brain.

Peale staggered and fell to the sidewalk a dying man, his pistol dropping from his hand as he fell.

Bull was tried and acquitted. He immediately left the Territory and returned for the first time yesterday. We talked over the terrible tragedy of his life. We crossed the street and stood on the same spot where he had met his foe.

"That," said he, "was my last difficulty. It made me cautious and I trust I shall never have another. Still I have nothing to regret and could do it again under similar circumstances."

He has been quite a wanderer since leaving Montana. Going from here to Cheyenne he remained there a year. From here he floated the White Pine and from thence he went to Chicago, where he engaged in business and married an estimable lady since dead, by whom he has two children living. From Chicago he went to Omaha where he engaged in the transfer business and made some money. Afterwards he went to the Black Hills and from thence to Denver where for the past three years he has been keeping the "Exchange and Turf" on the European plan.

He was surprised at the reports that had been circulated that he had been hung by a Vigilance Committee in Omaha and attributes the false report to the Editor of the Omaha *Bee*, with whom he had had some difficulty.

Mr. Bull finds a strange fascination in Helena and its surroundings. Possibly this is due to his tragic memories connected with the place. He proposes to go to the eastern end of the Northern Pacific RR and follow it westward till the converging lines meet at Helena, when he thinks that he will pitch his tent once more in this city, and end his eventful career among those scenes which have been indellibly stamped upon his memory.

[XII]

Final Justice

I WAS DEPUTY MARSHAL under G. M. Pinney in Helena on the day of election when the colored folks first voted.[1] There was bitter feeling. The territorial legislature had passed an act prohibiting colored people from exercising the right of franchise conferred on them by the Constitutional amendment. Marshal Pinney received orders from Washington to see that the colored vote offered should be cast.

Neil Howie and John Featherstone were also on duty on that fateful election day as deputy marshals.

In the morning, about nine A.M., before the polls opened, I was riding a good horse. About the head of Main Street I heard a shot fired down the street. I went there in a few jumps and found a Negro, laying dead on the sidewalk. Got off my horse, handing the lines to a boy. There was a man in the middle of the street, six-shooter in hand, still smoking.

I asked who killed the Negro, a janitor, called "Nigger Sammy," and was told that was the man, with the gun. His name was Leech—a powerful brute—who was a mule skinner for Hugh Kirkendall. As he came up the street going to the polls he met this "Nigger Sam" and said to him: "You nigger son of a bitch! Are you going to vote today?"

The coon said: "I don't know, boss!"

"Well," said Leech, "I know that you won't."

[1] This incident is reconstructed partially from longhand copy and partially from a clipping from the *Helena Independent* for May 13, 1886.

Sam said: "I aint doin' nothin', Marsa," and throwing open his coat, added: "An' I aint got nothin'."

Leech shot him dead.

This happened on the site of the Cosmopolitan Hotel.

I then jumped for the murderer and grabbed his gun by the barrel, and we had a tussle. I wrenched the gun from him and held him up with his own six-shooter. The crowd around immediately took sides, some shouting, "Let him go—he only killed a nigger!" and others saying—"Hang him!"

I got Jim Brewer and another fellow, Burt, whose last name I don't remember,—two powerful men—to hold Leech on either side and we started for the lockup on Wood Street, having to fight our way through the excited mob. It took us an hour and a half to go two blocks. With my six-shooter in hand, I swore I would kill any man who interfered. But when we got to the old jail, I hadn't enough clothes left on me to dress a china doll.

Later in the day, a friend of mine, Mr. Goldberg, and several others, were talking in Mathews' Saloon about what a good arrest I had made and got away with the prisoner in good shape, when a big fellow called "Bad Card George," a sage brush gambler, came up and said X was a liar and a coward, and couldn't arrest a baby. Goldberg couldn't take his gas any longer, so he reached over to the bar, seized a champagne bottle, and knocked "Bad Card" out.

"Bad Card" went off and got his head tied up and went gunning after Goldberg, whose friends came to me and told me he had got into trouble for taking my part, and said I must take the fight off his hands.

I went on the war path and found him in front of Fargo's office, with his six-shooter in his hand, looking for Goldberg. He was swearing bloody vengeance. I got the drop on him, grabbed him, disarmed him, took him to Exchange Corner and turned him over to the gamblers who put him to bed, because I said I would have to kill him if he did not go. Next morning, I gave him his gun and told him to be a good boy in the future.

After all this trouble, Leech, the murderer, broke from jail with another desperate character I arrested, "Big Nick" Freyer, and was never captured and no reward was offered for his capture and he went unpunished.

Just previous to the murder of "Nigger Sam" by Leech, Helena was being overrun with bogus gold dust. The merchants called my attention to it and wanted me to find out who was making it—showed me samples of the dust and I told them to watch out who they got it from. I found that lots of it was circulated on the race track. I traced it up to "Big Nick" Freyer.

I went and found where he had hired a blacksmith shop for $5. an hour, for as many hours as he wanted it—and when he was through, turned it over to the blacksmith again —pulled the wool over his eyes by telling him that he was assaying some rock and wanted to be alone excepting a man he had blowing the bellows.

In this blacksmith shop I found crucibles, brass, etc., and a camp kettle full of his bogus dust which he had spilt.

I arrested "Big Nick" and got Bill Warfield to walk with the prisoner ahead of me so I could see if he threw anything overboard on his way to the cooler. He threw a gold sack away while going up Wood Street. I caught it and locked up "Big Nick." He was fortunate enough to escape at the same time Leech escaped.

At the time I arrested Leech for killing the colored boy, Sam, Bill Hynson was there and after the affair was all over, he claimed he had kept a man from killing me with a knife.[2] I took his word for it and thanked him. He then asked me to get him a position as night watchman and I told him I would see about it. I did not place much confidence in him and always thought his "medicine" was bad, and he came to me again in a few days after he had made the request and said he did not want the job as he had a better thing.

Jack Oliver was running a stage line to Confederate Gulch, and one evening when the stage came in, Hynson was around the stage and went with the driver to the barn.

Next morning Oliver told me he had lost a Henry rifle. I hunted around and got onto Hynson, who was hanging around a Chinawoman's house, about half his time, and sometimes slept in an unfinished house near Chinatown.

One morning before daylight Bob Hereford came to my room and told me that a Chinawoman had been murdered. I went immediately to the place and found her dead on the floor of her room. She had evidently been choked to death. Her drawers were tied around her neck in a hard knot.

I went hunting for my particular friend, Bill Hynson, and found him in the unfinished house, and I also found Oliver's rifle there. I arrested Hynson for stealing the gun, and sent him up for three months, but I could not fix the murder on him at the time, although he was guilty.

He afterwards went to Benton and got on the night watch. I told the good people there that he was no good, but they kept him employed.

I was kept busy, traveling up and down the river and I got a letter from Silver Bow, telling me that a watchmaker's store had been robbed. I also got a description of the stolen goods and the man suspected of the robbery.

[2] There are two versions of the Hynson (Hinson) story in the long-hand copy. In the one not used, Hynson attempts to knife X as Leech is taken to jail.

I had to go away and I put Hynson on the job and he found the man and the stolen goods. He turned the man loose and appropriated the gold nuggets and pins to his own use.

When I came back, I got after him, and made him give up. I found one nugget with a lady friend of his. I got most of the property back from the Silver Bow man.

Hynson turned out to be a very bad man and the citizens of Benton put up a job on him. He was told they were going to hang a man. He never asked who it was, or what it was for, but was solid for the hanging, and procured the rope and fixed the tripod, and reported everything ready for the hanging bee. He hired old Nigger Henry to dig a grave. The nigger said: "Who is dead, Massa Hynson?"

"Never mind," said Hynson. "I will furnish the corpse."

The party then went out to the bluffs, Hynson in the lead. When they arrived at the place, he asked who they were going to hang. They told him, Bill Hynson, and it kind of knocked the wind out of him.

He was found the next day, hanging to his own tripod, and the darkey said: "Dat's de man what said he would furnish de corpse."

Appendices

APPENDIX I

Impressions of "X." Beidler

BY WILLIAM RANDALL (1869)

I WAS ASKED by my friend, Col. L. M. Black, to come to Montana to take charge of his business during his absence East, after a short consultation, I decided to go at once and the next day found me on my journey. At Omaha I could not purchase a ticket to Bozeman, as it was then unknown and Corinne, Utah, was as far as I could go by Rail, and from there to Helena by Coach, so I took only money enough to pay my fare to Helena, thinking it was near Corinne. What was my surprise on entering the ticket office, to find that it was several hundred miles to Helena and still nothing of *Bozeman.* However, after counting my fare to Helena I had *one 5 cent piece left,* and the Agent, counting after me, threw out a $10.00 bill as *counterfeit.* Heavens! thought I was a *goner.*

Just at that moment a short, heavy-set gentleman came in, had on a Buffalo over coat, the first I had ever seen, looked like a bear. I had often read of Road Agents, thought this must be the Captain, he had a Shot Gun and a belt with two large Pistols and a knife around him. I could not see his eyes until he removed his cap, when I found they were not only bent on me, but seemed to *pierce* clear through. However, rough as he looked, I thought I could detect in him a *kind* eye, even if it was *piercing*. He remarked that there were a good many counterfeits being brought to the country by *Tenderfeet* these days and that pretty soon, you would hear something *drop*. I did not know what either *Tenderfeet* or *dropping* meant at that time.

I asked if there was a Bank there, being informed there was, we walked up and with much joy found my money good. On getting in the coach for my long ride, it was with an aching heart and an empty stomach accompanied by the worst case of *Home Sickness* imaginable. Still was determined to reach Bozeman in some manner. I was the only Passenger but to my great *surprise* as well as *fear* this same short, Rough looking man, with his Pistols and Gun, mounted the Box at the outskirts of the town and seemed to be on intimate terms with the driver, and pretty soon another just as rough looking a character, mounted the Box and like the other, was greeted as a friend, remarking, "We have a *soft thing* of it this trip."

Right *then* and *there* I considered myself just as good as dead. *I,* of course, was that same *Soft thing,* with only *One 5 cent piece.* How I did want those fellows to *know it* on top. I sat and trembled for miles, and at every good looking place to hide a man, I expected to be *there* and *then* hid, and forever, too, and to confirm my suspicions, at every such place, there would be some kind of mysterious movements on top of the coach.

We moved along alright until noon when we stopped for dinner. The short, little man was the first one down, and taking a flask from his enormous pocket, passed it to me. Of course, I thought it was drugged in order to kill me more easily and I concluded to *take it* and be killed easy, so I took a *good one.* He says, "Now we will go to dinner." I told him I did not wish any. He says, "It is a long way to supper and *sand* didn't digest easy." I told him I had only *one nickel* left, *was busted* although I had on pretty good clothes. Says he; "Where in h—— are you going?"

"To Bozeman," says I.

Looking me over again, he says, "Who do you know in Bozeman?"

"L. M. Black is the only man I know in the Territory. Know him?"

"Yes. Come in get your dinner."

I never felt so relieved in my life, would at any rate die with a full stomach, which was some consolation in my present condition. After dinner, I told him if I should live to reach Bozeman I would pay him for his kindness. *"Shut up,"* was the only reply.

Before starting, he purchased a large size Basket and filled it with provisions of almost every description, a whole sack of watermelons and about 20 bottles of California Wine, placed them on the inside of the coach and appointed me as *Quarter Master in chief,* while he would prefer riding out side. I was completely *changed* and as I now had a *friend,* I would willingly have fought Road Agents with him, with only a *club,* but he furnished me with a gun, and I felt, even almost wished, the Road Agents would call on us, so that I could show my new found friend how I could, and would fight.

He soon found out all about *me,* but I could get nothing out of him, only "X is my name. Tell Col. Black you met X on the road, give him a *shake* for me." He would not hear of my paying him for his kindness. He would simply say, "Don't mention it, somebody might hear it, which would give you away." On reaching Pleasant Valley, he bid me adieu, with wishes for my welfare and to be sure to keep my *nickel* for luck.

X. Beidler: Vigilante

After reaching Helena and finding Col. Black, I soon found out all about X, and who he was, and it was a few years afterwards that we met in Bozeman and I was perfectly surprised to see that he knew my face and name, the moment his eagle eyes met mine—the recognition was mutual and for months afterwards, we occupied the same room, he being then acting dep. U. S. Marshal, special detective and has been the means, above all others, of clearing eastern Montana of rough characters. Here, there, and *every where,* like the dutchman's Flee [flea]—where you think he is, he ain't. Have tried night after night to find him asleep but could never with the faintest whisper, say X, but what he would answer in a *second.* Have had many ups and downs with him in the early days of Bozeman and he is today, as he ever has been, the same genial, good hearted X. Beidler.

Tribute to X. Beidler

BY COL. A. K. McCLURE

(Author of *Three Thousand Miles*
Through the Rocky Mountains)

"THERE IS one who figures as conspicuously in the history of the Vigilantes as did Plummer in his reign of terror. Some twelve years ago I was accustomed to meeting on the streets of Chambersburg, Pennsylvania, a young man named John X. Beidler. His frugal wants were supplied by the manufacture of brooms, and finally, he mixed the best cock-tails and juleps at the neighborhood summer resort. He was as amiable and unoffending a lad as the community could furnish, and his jolly, genial humor made him a favorite with all who knew him. Although he had attained his majority, he was scarcely five feet six inches in height and was far below the average man in physical power.

He finally wandered West in search of fortune, and soon after the advent of Plummer came "X," the name by which he is universally known in Montana. Thus the bane and the antidote were close upon each other. Strong in his inherent love of honesty, a stranger to fear, not powerful, but quick as thought in his actions, and firm in his purpose as the eternal mountains around him, he naturally entered promptly and earnestly into the effort to restore order and safety to society. That little was expected of him when he first cast his lot with the stern reformers is not surprising; but his tireless perseverance, unfaltering courage and singular skill in thwarting the plans of the common enemy, soon made him the chief pillar of the organization, and the unspeakable terror of every desperado. This diminutive man, without family or property to defend, has himself arrested scores of the most powerful villains, and executed in open day, an equal number under the direction of that wonderful, dreaded, unseen power that surrounded the hasty scaffold. So expert is he with his faithful pistol that the most scientific of rogues have repeatedly attempted in vain to get the "drop" on him. Quick as a flash, his pistol is drawn, cocked in the drawing, and presented at the man, with the stern command: "Hands up, sir!" and the work is done.

At one time, without aid, he arrested six of the most desperate thieves in a body, all well armed and marched them before him, to prison. "Hands up, gents!" was the first intimation they had from him that he had business with them and submission was the only course of safety. Had any one of them attempted to reach toward his belt, he would have fallen that moment. There were citizens close by; and how many of them, if any, were sworn to protect and ready to aid Beidler, he knew—while the prisoners did not. This indefinite, unseen, immeasurable power seems to have stricken the most courageous thieves and murderers nerveless, when its sudden and fatal grasp was thrown around them. They would fight scores of men for their lives in any ordinary attempt to arrest them, but they seemed weakened when the citizens confronted them in the name of Public Safety. No formalities were known. No process was read bearing the high seal of the Courts. When or where the dread summons of the great, unseen tribunal would come, none could conjecture. The sleeping companion of the desperado in some distant ranch would probably drink and breakfast with him and then paralyze him by the notice —"You're wanted—business in Virginia."

In no instance did any of the lawless characters arrested by the Vigilantes ever fire a pistol in their defenses, even when they knew that death was inevitable. In most cases the opportunity to do so was but slight but under ordinary circumstances, the closest chances would be taken, to effect escape. From X no criminal ever got away. To have attempted it would have been to hasten death. So much did the desperadoes respect as well as fear him, that most of them condemned to die at his hands, committed their last requests to him and with him they have been sacred.

Order and public safety have been restored but he still has employment in his favorite line. He comes and goes but none but himself know his errand. "What's up, X?" is a query that is generally answered: "After tracks," and "Don't know," is his usual reply to all questions as to his route or time of departure. He has travelled along every highway and settlement in Montana, prospected many of the unexplored regions and is always ready, without escort or aid, to pursue a criminal, wherever he may seek refuge. His career has indeed been most remarkable and his escape, unharmed, through his innumerable conflicts with the worst of men, seems almost wholly miraculous.

While there is a thief, a murderer, a defaulter or a savage to disturb the peace of Montana, he will remain the most efficient messenger of justice known in the mountain gold regions. He has lost none of his genial, kindly nature by his long service as minister of vengeance upon the lawless.

X. Beidler Captures Harry Arden

(Author Unknown)

EARLY in 1875 I was a boy on a ranch in the Missouri Valley. Two men with a team met me on the road one day and one of them asked me if there was a man working in that vicinity named Harry Vincent. I said, "Yes. He is herding sheep." And I pointed to where he could be seen about a mile away. The man asked me to go with him and as we went along, he, walking with a limping gait, would occasionally call my attention to the sheep, or something in the distance, pointing with his stick. I thought he was some country duffer interested in sheep.

When we reached the herd, X made some remark to the herder about the sheep and turning so as to face him, he said: "Your name's Harry Arden, is it not?" I never before saw a man look so surprised. "Well, I'm X. Beidler and I came out to take you to Helena." The man said he couldn't leave the sheep. "Oh! this boy will look after the sheep," said X. Then X put handcuffs on the man. I was all eyes but I couldn't tell where in the world those handcuffs came from. Taking a revolver from Arden's hip, X knocked the caps off. It was a muzzle loader and he handed the revolver to me.

We went to the house and Arden complained that he couldn't pick up his belongings with the handcuffs on. "Get what you can," said X "and let the rest go." Finally, X considerately unlocked the cuff from one wrist and sat down on a stool. Soon after the man went to turn down his pillow to roll it into his bedding as I supposed, but X must have detected something else, for quick as a flash, he had whipped out his revolver and had it at Arden's head. "Touch that and you are a dead man. Why, you are one of the biggest fools I ever saw. I have half a notion to shoot you just for luck!" The handcuffs went back on and X reached under the pillow and handed me another revolver.

Story of a Fabulous Beaver

(From the *Bozeman Times,* November 2, 1877)

U. S. Dep. Marshal, J. X. Beidler, just in from Stillwater, dropped into our office and related the following tough story.

A large number of men are still scouting for Gen'l Howard in that section of the country, being ignorant that the Nez Percé war had been ended by Gen'l Miles, and amongst them he met a man who said he had just got away with a big beaver that weighed more than a hundred pounds. The varmint, the man stated, came at him hand over fist, and struck him a terrible blow on the nose with a big wolf trap which it had fastened to its foot, but he finally got away with it single handed, after a terrible encounter of about two hours. It proved to be valuable property, for he sold the tail for a rudder for a government boat, and the last seen of the boat, it was about two miles in the lead of the balance. X says the party lit out for Tongue River after his encounter and could not be induced to go within half a mile of a patch of willows for fear the beaver would take him in. He saw the skin of the animal and said he took it for a Buffalo Robe and asked the man where he killed that big Buffalo. The man turned and said child like and bland, "Why, that's my beaver skin."

We didn't want to be too inquisitive, for we pride ourselves on our knowledge of the beaver, but finally asked what became of the hide? He said a gang of Howard's scouts were sleeping under it, using it for a cover.

Tribute to Col. Wilbur F. Sanders

(Author Unknown)

SENATOR Wilbur F. Sanders was ever aggressive and independent, and his battle cry in the heat of strife was: "No quarter." He was equally at ease in the Senate of the United States, an assembly of the bar, or a banquet, the miners' court, or the Supreme Court. In his mind all things were upon the same plane, and he showed the same intense spirit in a ward primary to nominate an alderman, or a national convention to choose a candidate for president of the Republic.

Let us dwell on a trait all—especially students—should emulate. The favorite abode of Senator Sanders was his library; his reading embraced the best authors of England and America; knowledge was his treasure house; his memory of everything was wonderful; and his vocabulary was unsurpassed by any person in the state. His style was unique, the meaning of every sentence was clear and his ideas and illustrations were clothed in felicitous phrases. He handled the keen weapons of logic and satire with dexterity.

Hon. William Scallon, who prepared the obituary of Senator Sanders for the American Bar Association, wrote: "He was noted for his mastery of the English language and for his eloquence, his power of invective, wit and sarcasm." This keenness of intellect and his powers of speech called forth from Robert G. Ingersoll, to whom he was opposed in the trial of a noted case, that remark that "Sanders was the keenest blade he had ever crossed."

He studied diligently the meaning of words and the rules of grammar and rhetoric, and the sentences of a letter on a common topic were framed as correctly as a document of the highest concern. In oral arguments and informal talks, he sought likewise to be exact in the use of terms and state his propositions with precision. He was not content with his *erudition* in this regard, but consulted often treatises and lexicons to improve his diction and strengthen his intellectual forces, and the lesson taught by this illustrious exemplar should be remembered.

The observation of Cicero in the essay on the Republic is worthy of repetition: "Nor, indeed, is there anything in which human virtue can more closely resemble the divine powers, than in establishing new states, or in preserving those already established." It was the rare distinction of Senator Sanders to illustrate both.

THE WESTERN FRONTIER LIBRARY

of which *X. Beidler: Vigilante* is Number 8, was started in 1953 by the University of Oklahoma Press. It is designed to introduce today's readers to the exciting events of our frontier past and to some of the memorable writings about them. The following list is complete as of the date of publication of this volume:

1. Prof. Thomas J. Dimsdale. *The Vigilantes of Montana.* With an introduction by E. DeGolyer.
2. A. S. Mercer. *The Banditti of the Plains.* With a foreword by William H. Kittrell.
3. Pat F. Garrett. *The Authentic Life of Billy, the Kid.* With an introduction by J. C. Dykes.
4. Yellow Bird (John Rollin Ridge). *The Life and Adventures of Joaquín Murieta.* With an introduction by Joseph Henry Jackson.
5. Lewis H. Garrard. *Wah-to-yah and the Taos Trail.* With an introduction by A. B. Guthrie, Jr.
6. Charles L. Martin. *A Sketch of Sam Bass, the Bandit.* With an introduction by Ramon F. Adams.
7. Washington Irving. *A Tour on the Prairies.* With an introduction by John Francis McDermott.
8. *X. Beidler: Vigilante.* Edited by Helen Fitzgerald Sanders in collaboration with William H. Bertsche, Jr. With a foreword by A. B. Guthrie, Jr.

University of Oklahoma Press : Norman